MOUNTAINEERING ESSAYS

Mountaineering Essays

John Muir

Edited and introduced by

Richard F. Fleck

THE UNIVERSITY OF UTAH PRESS

Salt Lake City

LIBRARY OF CONGRESS CATALOGING-IN-PUBLICATION DATA
Muir, John, 1838–1914.
     Mountaineering essays / John Muir ; edited and
introduced by Richard F. Fleck
        p.   cm.
     Originally published: Salt Lake City : Peregrine
Smith Books, 1989, in series: Peregrine Smith literary
naturalists. With new introd.
     ISBN 0-87480-544-9 (alk. paper)
     1. Mountaineering—West (U.S.) 2. West (U.S.)
—Description and travel. I. Fleck, Richard F.,
1937– . II. Title.
[GV199.42.W39M84 1997]
796.52'2'0978—dc21   97-15973

CONTENTS

Introduction vii

The Tuolumne Camp 1

A Near View of the High Sierra 23

Prayers in Higher Mountain Temples, or
A Geologist's Winter Walk 55

A Perilous Night on Shasta's Summit 65

The South Dome 91

Mountain Thoughts 99

An Ascent of Mount Rainier 107

The Stickeen River 117

Glenora Peak 133

My Sled-Trip on the Muir Glacier 145

First Ascent of Herald Island 167

INTRODUCTION
"They wear many spiritual robes"

IN early October 1983 I first set eyes on Mount Rainier, some ninety-five years after John Muir's three-day ascent to its 14,410 feet summit known as Columbia Crest. I had just come from Stockton, California where I had examined the unpublished notes and journals of Muir for several weeks. My tired eyes were in dire need of the relief of a mountain wilderness. Mount Rainier, with its fifty glaciers kissing the sky, was just the right place. It is one thing to read Muir's fascinating accounts of crossing rough glaciers with crevasses and streaks of mountain debris, and it is quite another to heed Muir's call to go out and experience the mountains. As I hiked up Rainier's Paradise Glacier with its scores of eery and gurgling ice caves, rocks tore loose from the flanks of the mountain and cracked down sheer cliffs to the wrinkled ice not far from where I stopped to rest. I began to sense a living presence and planetary change by spending time on what Muir called "God's ice tool."

Reaching the top of Paradise Glacier on that chilly clear October morning with a fine view of icy Mount Adams and level-topped Mount St. Helens to the south, I continued my ascent up an arm of Cowlitz Glacier with its dark and gaping crevasses. When I arrived at the edge of a jagged black lava ridge, I peered up to what is called "Muir Camp" nestled under higher reddish lava ridges above the 9,000 feet level of Mount

MOUNTAINEERING ESSAYS

Rainier. And then mist rolled in, followed by strands of thick grey clouds. "Muir Camp" blurred out of sight. Knowing I must get down the mountain quickly for fear of getting lost on the steep slopes of the glacier, I carefully picked my route down into the lower valleys barely visible in thickening clouds. By the time I reached the comforts of a hotel fireplace crackling with red cedar logs, I had gained some measure of Muir's exquisite joy of being in the mountains where human spirit and primal nature fuse. John Muir's effective translation of this joy makes him one of the world's foremost writers of the mountaineering essay, truly a literary genre in its own right. Each of the eleven essays selected in this volume has a rich tincture of spiritual, philosophical, descriptive, and adventuresome elements.

I developed an early interest in Muir when, as a ranger in Rocky Mountain National Park twenty-five years ago, I had occasion to meet Mrs. Esther Mills, widow of Enos Mills, in Estes Park, Colorado. She told me of her husband's ardent desire to preserve a portion of the northern Colorado Rockies as a national park. Her husband met John Muir back in 1907 and was encouraged by Muir to continue his good efforts. In 1913 Mills wrote Muir that 716 square miles had been recommended for the creation of Rocky Mountain National Park. Mills and Muir knew all too well that mountains need to be preserved in order that they may preserve us. Having stood on the inspiriting summits of Mount Katahdin, Maine, or Longs Peak, Colorado, or Mount Fuji, Japan at various stages of my own life, I have returned again and again to the fresh and vital writings of John Muir.

INTRODUCTION

Born in Dunbar, Scotland in 1838, Muir, as a young lad, delighted in the wild. In his *Story of My Boyhood and Youth*, Muir relates that he used to climb up the crumbling peaks of old Dunbar Castle. "That I did not fall," he writes, "and finish my rock-scrambling in those adventurous boyhood days seems now a reasonable wonder."

In 1849 the Muirs left Scotland for the wilds of Wisconsin where, as Linnie Marsh Wolfe states in her biography *Son of the Wilderness: The Life of John Muir*, "Had the future naturalist had all the world from which to choose as his training-ground, he could hardly have found a richer treasure house than Fountain Lake, the boggy meadow, and the woods that embosomed them." But all was not joy on their Wisconsin farm near Portage; Daniel Muir, John's father, was a stern, Bible-preaching fundamentalist who insisted on long hard hours of work in the fields, in digging wells even if it spelled potential danger to his own flesh and blood. Spare time, Daniel believed, should not be spent in the wilds looking at birds and plants and it should not be spent reading vain books or trying to invent vain machinery. All is vanity except for the reading of Scripture and attempting to know the Lord.

Muir's father caused two traits to develop in his son as a result of insisting on hard labor and negative preaching: an iron endurance, and an insatiable curiosity, two traits which characterize almost every mountaineer. The more John Muir read and wandered about the woodlands (without his father's permission), the more curious he became about man, nature and God. Quite fortunately Muir left his household at the age of twenty-two for Madison with some machines he had invented for waking up early (to read non-biblical literature) and for measuring time. He entered them in the Wisconsin State Fair and gained instant recognition, which led to his entering the University of Wisconsin to study, among other things, geology with Dr. Ezra Slocum Carr, and the Classics with Dr. James Davie Butler who instructed him to keep a journal in the manner of Ralph Waldo Emerson. Young Muir had to work his way through college as his stubborn father would not support him.

Though Muir earned no "degree" at Wisconsin, he was introduced to the glacial theories of Agassiz, and to the transcendentalism of Ralph Waldo Emerson and Henry David Thoreau. These two authors were to become the two most important literary influences on John Muir. Years later in 1871 in Yosemite, Muir had the splendid occasion of meeting Emerson in person and of corresponding with him years afterwards. While he did not meet Thoreau (who died while Muir was still a student at Madison), he did become acquainted with his complete writings which he read carefully through and through.

After recovering from a tragic accident which nearly blinded his right eye, Muir vowed to spend the rest of his days studying God's unwritten Bible, nature, which he called the University of the Wilderness. That iron endurance of his gained during his boyhood exhibited itself forcefully when he walked a thousand miles in 1867 from Indiana to Florida to study flora and fauna. In the southern Appalachians we get our first hint of Muir's

INTRODUCTION

special love for mountains. He writes in *A Thousand
Mile Walk*, "Most glorious billowing mountain scenery
[Unaka Mountains of Tennessee]. Made many a halt at
open places to take breath and to admire. The road, in
many places cut into the rock, goes winding about among
the knobs and gorges. Dense growth of asters, liatris
[Vanilla Plant], and grapevines."

Shortly after John Muir arrived in California in 1868
to continue studying at the University of the Wilderness,
he quickly became attracted to the alluring, always shining Sierra Nevada. He spent the summer of 1868 and
the spring of 1869 at Twenty Hill Hollow near the foothills of the Sierra. At the close of *A Thousand Mile
Walk* Muir fully explains the power of mountains and
his affinity for them:

> It may be asked, what have mountains fifty
> or a hundred miles away to do with Twenty Hill
> Hollow? To lovers of the wild, these mountains
> are not a hundred miles away. Their spiritual
> power and the goodness of the sky make them
> near, as a circle of friends. They rise as portion
> of the hilled walls of the Hollow. You cannot
> feel yourself out of doors; plain, sky, and moun-
> tains ray beauty which you feel. You bathe in
> these spirit-beams, turning round and round, as
> if warming at a camp-fire. Presently you lose
> consciousness of your own separate existence: you
> blend with the landscape, and become part and
> parcel of nature.

During the summer of 1869 Muir gained deeper
knowledge of the mountains by being a shepherd for

MOUNTAINEERING ESSAYS

Mr. Delaney, who fortunately allowed him to do a good bit of wandering. He kept a journal which became the basis of *My First Summer in the Sierra* (1911). The book abounds with commentary on "mountain manuscripts" which are part of nature's hieroglyphic language. The young Scotsman learned to decipher this language with ease, and through it he was able to determine that Yosemite was not formed by a cataclysmic event as state geologist Josiah Whitney insisted, but was carved gradually by ancient glaciers. If only he could find remnants of these glaciers in the high Sierra, his hypothesis would have greater credibility. Because Muir believed (as did Emerson and Thoreau) that nature speaks to the human spirit in symbolic language, these mountains were not just mountains but living testimony to God's continual work and presence. As Muir writes, "The place seemed holy, where one might hope to see God." Such a sense of a landscape's religiosity is also seen in writers like Willa Cather in her New Mexican novel, *Death Comes for the Archbishop*, and in Edward Abbey's *Desert Solitaire* in which he asks of Utah canyonlands, "Is this at last the *locus Dei*? There are enough cathedrals and temples and altars here for a Hindu pantheon of divinities."

Between 1869 and 1871 Muir searched the high country of the Sierra for ice, moving ice, a *mer de glace* which would confirm his intuitive belief that God was still at work. On October 8, 1872, Muir wrote his old friend from Madison (who had moved with her husband to California), Mrs. Ezra Slocum Carr, about a discovery he had made the previous October. He had come across

INTRODUCTION

a muddy stream he had never before seen. The mud was entirely mineral in composition and "fine as flour—like mud from a fine grit grindstone." He followed the stream up its banks along a moraine at the base of Mount Lyell (at the eastern edge of what is today, thanks to Muir, Yosemite National Park). His narrative continues:

> When I scrambled to the top of the moraine I saw what seemed to be a huge snowbank four or five hundred yards in length by half a mile in width. Embedded in its stained and furrowed surface were stones and dirt like that of which the moraine was built. Dirtstained lines curved across the snowbank from side to side, and when I observed that these curved lines coincided with the curved moraine, and that the stones and dirt were most abundant near the bottom of the bank, I shouted, "A living glacier!" These bent dirt lines show that the ice is flowing in its different parts with unequal velocity, and these embedded stones are journeying down to be built into the moraine, and they gradually become more abundant as they approach the moraine because there the motion is slower.

With the encouragement of Mrs. Carr, Muir put such observations in the form of seven scientific articles known as "Studies in the Sierra," published in the *Overland Monthly* beginning in 1874. "Studies in the Sierra" gained Muir national recognition—not to mention financial income—but placed him in the midst of the ire and contempt of Josiah Whitney. As time passed, however, Muir's views gained more and more support until his complete exoneration by the geological establishment. Today, of course, Muir is considered to be one of America's pioneer glaciologists.

Muir's studies of mountains and glaciers continued with his travels to Alaska beginning in 1879 and continuing for twenty years. Alaska, he would come to discover, is the birthplace of future yosemites because of the gigantic, living, carving glaciers forming bergs dramatically in the coastal waters of misty fiords. He developed an intense love and fascination for these Alaskan glaciers because they so beautifully testified to God's ways. What more beautiful proof could there be for his intuitive conviction that out of destruction comes a new and glorious creation. Nothing could be more forcefully destructive than millions of tons of grinding ice which crunch and pulverize the flanks of a mountain. But nothing could be more beautiful than a resulting flower-carpeted, lake-studded alpine valley. It is no wonder his Alaskan friends, the Thlinkit Indians, called him "Ice Chief." He was in constant search of undiscovered glaciers tucked away in some unexplored recess. One such glacier bears his name today.

Muir did not write his first book *(The Mountains of California,* 1894) until he was almost sixty. But between the age of fifty-six and his death at age seventy-six (1914), Muir either wrote or was working on *Our National Parks* (1901), *My First Summer in the Sierra* (1911), *Yosemite* (1912), *The Story of My Boyhood and Youth* and *A Thousand Mile Walk to the Gulf* (1913), and *Travels in Alaska* (1915), his yet-to-be-published aphorisms and an incompleted book on mountaineering. He had had so

INTRODUCTION

many fascinating experiences in his life that his wife Louie Wanda Strentzel (whom he married in 1880) encouraged him to set down his thoughts in books for the public to enjoy. Some of the books written in the "scribble den" at Martinez had a political cause, such as *Our National Parks*. Muir believed that we must develop a system of national parks throughout America in order that future generations may be spiritually inspired. Both his founding of the Sierra Club in 1892 and his taking President Theodore Roosevelt on a camping trip in the Sierra in 1902 certainly helped this cause. Muir naturally gave his wholehearted support to conservationists like Enos Mills, who lived to see the formation of the National Park Service in 1916. Other books consisted of pure and joyous description of Sequoia forests, Douglass squirrels, water ouzels and mountain scenery *(The Mountains of California, Yosemite)*. In *The Cruise of the Corwin* (1918), one of three books collected from the writings of John Muir by William Frederick Badè, we can see a new side of John Muir—that of a social critic. He was deeply angered by the cheap and ruthless commercialization of Eskimos for the sole purpose of lucrative fur trade. The Eskimos of Saint Lawrence Island in the Bering Straits were destroyed by greed. In the interests of gaining more and more seal furs, white traders gave the Eskimo hunters repeating rifles and whiskey. The repeating rifles killed off the seal population and the whiskey made the Eskimos listless and dependent. After Muir witnessed a village of the dead where hundreds of arctic natives died of starvation, Muir lashed out:

MOUNTAINEERING ESSAYS

> Unless some aid be extended by our government which claims these people, in a few years at most every soul of them will have vanished from the face of the earth; for, even where alcohol is left out of the count, the few articles of food, clothing, guns, etc., furnished by the traders, exert a degrading influence, making them less self-reliant, and less skillful as hunters. They seem susceptible of civilization, and well deserve the attention of our government.

Since thousands of people first read this forceful commentary in the form of a letter to the *San Francisco Evening Bulletin*, Muir may very well have helped shape future governmental policies in the American arctic.

Turning our attention specifically to John Muir's mountaineering essays, as previously mentioned, he was at work on planning a mountaineering book very late in life. Muir had notes on the world's mountain ranges from the Swiss Alps (which he visited in 1893) to the California Sierra, to the Asian Himalayas (which he visited in 1902). Muir had an excellent collection of mountaineering books in his personal library at Martinez. Some of the titles included: J. Norman Collie, *Climbing on the Himalaya and Other Mountain Ranges*, Sir Martin Conway, *The Bolivian Andes: A Record of Climbing and Exploration*, John M. Phillips, *Campfires in the Canadian Rockies*, Hudson Stuck, *The Ascent of Denali* (Mount McKinley), Henry David Thoreau, *The Maine Woods* (containing his ascent of Mount Ktaadn, now spelled Katahdin), Edward Whymper, *Scrambles Amongst the Alps in the Years 1860-1869*, Walter Dwight

INTRODUCTION

Wilcox, *The Rockies of Canada*, and Andrew Wilson, *The Abode of Snow* (which is the Sanskrit meaning of "Himalaya"). Muir himself, of course, was a skilled mountaineer and had made many miraculous ascents of his own. In *Nature in American Literature*, Norman Foerster writes, "Never, perhaps, has there been such a complete mountaineer and glacier-climber as he, unsurpassed alike in skill, in knowledge, in passionate enjoyment."

For his own mountaineering book, Muir wished to include, in addition to adventure, such descriptive features as alpine soil beds, ancient glaciers and glacial denudation, living glaciers, and mountain sculpture. The essays collected in this volume are, hopefully, ones which Muir himself would have picked as they do encompass the topics of his outline and contain the best of his prose. Writing came hard for John Muir and that is why he turned to Henry David Thoreau for an accomplished literary model. As Michael Cohen states in his essay "Stormy Sermons," included in the book *The World of John Muir*, "If Emerson had been the mentor for a young man who had left the family farm, Thoreau was the superior craftsman to whom a serious writer who wanted to say a word for nature would turn." If one peruses Muir's personal set of the writings of Thoreau in twenty volumes contained at the Holt-Atherton Pacific Center for Western Studies in Stockton, California, he will see Muir's pencil marks and marginal notes in each and every volume. At the back of Volume III, *The Maine Woods*, is Muir's own index written in pencil, which includes the topics of mountains and mountaineering. When Muir wrote, he turned to his field notes and journals for vital information. From field notes came his first pencil draft which received many corrections and emendations. From this draft came an ink copy which again was corrected and emendated. This penned draft led to a typed copy which again was corrected to his liking until a final typed copy was ready for the publisher. Such a process can be seen by examining the manuscript versions of his published essay "An Ascent of Mount Rainier," included in this volume.

The mountaineering essay is a literary genre in its own right. One can go to the Classics and find Petrarch's "Ascent of Mount Ventoux" or to the recently published work of Peter Matthiessen, *Snow Leopard*, to discover a type of literature which is as philosophical, as exciting, and as aesthetically pleasing as the best of any other genre. What makes such literature a genre of its own? *Mountains*. Mountains are the key to discovery, not necessarily of new geographic domain but of the inner human being. Be the Frobisher and Henry Hudson of your own dark continent, Thoreau advises. For Petrarch and Peter Matthiessen the mountains are indeed a source of discovery, and to journey up their slopes is to journey deep into the human psyche. John Muir was also a master of the mountaineering essay because he was able to maintain a careful and subtle balance between the physical and symbolic aspects of ascending, rescuing the injured, or observing the sublimity of mountains. They were for him a supreme test and affirmation of the human spirit.

Turning to the selections found in this volume, the

INTRODUCTION

first collection of journal entries, "The Tuolumne Camp," comes from Muir's 1869 experience of shepherding for Mr. Delaney. Though this journal was written during his first summer in the high country, it was embellished some forty years later for publication of *My First Summer in the Sierra* in 1911. One can sense Muir's intense desire to know the mountains if only he could break away from those sheep. Mr. Delaney was an understanding man and relieved the young Scotsman every now and then. By September 1 he does manage to climb Mount Dana where he takes time to enjoy not only grand and sweeping views but also delicate plants clinging to crumbling tops of moraines. On September 7 Muir ascends the topmost spire of Cathedral Peak where he is most receptive to a spiritual presence. He doesn't climb mountains to be "egotistic" but to be inspired and to take joy in each snowfield, each flower, and each rock that he can observe.

"A Near View of the High Sierra" comes from his first book, *The Mountains of California*. The actual experience took place in October 1872 when Muir met three artists, William Keith (with whom he would have a life-long friendship), Benoni Irwin, and Thomas Ross, who wished to paint alpine scenery from a location which wasn't too vast to behold. He led them along the upper Tuolumne River to a spot they couldn't resist. Muir, leaving his companions, sought the higher grounds of Mount Ritter. In this essay we can experience some of Muir's most exciting prose depicting his dilemma of being stuck at 12,800 feet on the icy slopes of Ritter with nowhere to go except to his doom. We die with him up there until a sixth sense takes hold of him and shows him the way. We share his exaltation and can, I think, truly understand that mountains are more than mountains. Stephen Fox, in his recent book *John Muir and His Legacy*, believes that on the summits of the Sierra Muir found "a degree of psychic integration previously unknown to him."

"Prayers in Higher Mountain Temples" or "A Geologist's Winter Walk" comes from *Steep Trails*, edited by William Frederic Badè and published in 1918. It was first written in 1873 in the form of a letter to a friend (Mrs. Jeanne Carr) and was occasioned by his returning to the Sierra Nevada in late 1872 after a stay in San Francisco where his feet had become deadened by city sidewalks. In this essay Muir describes his bad fall, his embarrassment, and his ultimate rejuvenation in which alpine "sun-love" made him strong again.

"A Perilous Night on Shasta's Summit" really consists of two separate episodes, the first taking place in October 1874 and the second in late April and early May 1875. The essay itself was first written for publication in a collection of various nature essays by different authors and illustrated by William Keith under the title *Picturesque California* (1888). William Frederic Badè included it in *Steep Trails* in 1918. Unlike his father who considered storms, in Calvinistic fashion, to be punishments of God, Muir delighted in storms even if they froze and fatigued his body. For him to have spent a night nearly frozen and volcanically roasted to death on the upper slopes of Mount Shasta was simply an exhilarating experience; one can hardly imagine Emer-

INTRODUCTION

son or even Thoreau coming away from such a howling alpine blizzard with a sense of delight.

The last two sections of *High Sierra*, "The South Dome" and "Mountain Thoughts," both come out of Muir's Yosemite days of the 1870s. He scaled the South Dome on November 10, 1875, following George Anderson's route up the sheer, snowy face, but with little boasting: "I therefore pushed on and gained the top." This essay most assuredly covers one of the topics of his intended mountaineering book, mountain sculpture. "The South Dome" comes from *The Mountains of California*. "Mountain Thoughts" are a series of miniature essays written probably in the early 1870s and collected, along with many other selections, by Linnie Marsh Wolfe in 1938 under the title *John of the Mountains: The Unpublished Journals of John Muir*. These reflective thoughts give balance to the exciting narratives of climbing to the summits of Cathedral Peak, Ritter, Shasta, or the South Dome. In a sense, they represent a different kind of climbing, climbing inscapes of the mind in which the presence of mountains is felt in a more subtle and spiritual way.

"An Ascent of Mount Rainier" returns us to the excitement of icy slopes, physical exhaustion, and magnificent views. After spending a windy night at what is today called "Muir Camp," Muir and company climbed on to the Columbia Crest of this rugged, frozen volcano in August 1888. The climb revitalized him after a long spell at his fruit ranch in Martinez. His wife Louie insisted he return to the wilds to pick up his spirit. Muir and his travelling companions, including the artist Wil-

MOUNTAINEERING ESSAYS

liam Keith, could not have chosen a more challenging peak than this, as it is now called, "Little Piece of Alaska" in Washington. The essay originally appeared in *Steep Trails* thirty years after the climb, in 1918. Inasmuch as the manuscript draft of it is included with his mountaineering book outline and other notes, I feel certain it would have been part of his intended volume.

The next three selections, "The Stickeen River," "Glenora Peak," and "My Sled-Trip on the Muir Glacier," all come from the posthumously published *Travels in Alaska;* the first two are based on his 1879 excursion and the last on his trip of 1880. In "The Stickeen River" Muir shows us another side of himself—a man who must pay dearly for his impatience with an amateur mountaineer. Fortunately, Muir's gruffness and impatience, after Samuel Young's bad fall, are replaced with compassion, concern, and self-remorse. One should, I suppose, read Samuel Young's account of the same episode in *Alaska Days with John Muir*. Certainly the "rescue narrative" is a significant and exciting part of mountaineering literature. "Glenora Peak" continues where the first essay leaves off. Muir seizes the opportunity of returning *by himself* to the same territory to climb Glenora Peak and witness some of the most inspiring and sublime landscapes of his entire life. "My Sled-Trip on the Muir Glacier" is largely concerned with living glaciers and their effect on landscapes of Glacier Bay, Alaska. Despite the hardships of snow-blindness, of falling into an icy, water-filled crevasse and shivering all night in a sleeping bag like a Jack London protagonist, Muir feels no ill effects; quite the contrary, he feels

INTRODUCTION

an inner contentment of having experienced at age fifty-two a meaningful arctic adventure.

In 1881 Muir boarded the *Corwin*, whose mission it was to search for the lost vessel *Jeannette* in Alaskan waters. The expedition afforded him the opportunity of studying the living glaciers of Alaska, of acquainting himself with Aleut, Eskimo, and Chukchi cultures, and of climbing arctic coastal mountains to scan the horizon for the *Jeannette*. Muir sent a series of letters as an arctic correspondent to the *San Francisco Evening Bulletin* which, along with other materials, were collected by William Frederic Badè in 1918 and published as *The Cruise of the Corwin;* "First Ascent of Herald Island" comes from this work. After some difficulty in finding an approach to this sheer granite block of an island, Muir succeeds in scaling the summit where he spends "one of the most impressive hours" of his life simply staring out over vast virgin landscapes to the icy north.

What can be said of John Muir's contributions to mountaineering literature? In her biography of John Muir, Linnie Marsh Wolfe relates that a young boy by the name of Samuel Merrill used to come to Martinez in the early 1890s and sit by the fire to listen to stories told by John Muir. Wolfe writes that on one evening, "being in a mystical mood, Muir related the story of the telepathic message that led him to Dr. Butler in the Yosemite. Also the summons that called him to his dying father. The boy asked him how he accounted for such strange happenings. Muir replied: 'Anyone who lives close to the mountains is sensitive to these things.' " When Muir climbed to the lofty summits of so many mountains in the Sierra, the Cascades, and Panhandle Alaska, surely his extrasensory perceptions were all the more heightened; this heightened or transcendental awareness is clearly conveyed in John Muir's mountaineering essays. Whether frozen in a below-zero blizzard on Mount Shasta or momentarily doomed on the treacherous slopes of Mount Ritter or exhilarated by the wondrous alpine ice-scapes from the top of Mount Rainier, Muir exalted in God's creation. No more apt words are there for John Muir than those of the biblical psalm, "I will lift up mine eyes unto the mountains whence cometh my strength."

Richard F. Fleck

MOUNTAINEERING ESSAYS

August 22. Clouds none, cool west wind, slight hoarfrost on the meadows. Carlo is missing; have been seeking him all day. In the thick woods between camp and the river, among tall grass and fallen pines, I discovered a baby fawn. At first it seemed inclined to come to me; but when I tried to catch it, and got within a rod or two, it turned and walked softly away, choosing its steps like a cautious, stealthy, hunting cat. Then, as if suddenly called or alarmed, it began to buck and run like a grown deer, jumping high above the fallen trunks, and was soon out of sight. Possibly its mother may have called it, but I did not hear her. I don't think fawns ever leave the home thicket or follow their mothers until they are called or frightened. I am distressed about Carlo. There are several other camps and dogs not many miles from here, and I still hope to find him. He never left me before. Panthers are very rare here, and I don't think any of these cats would dare touch him. He knows bears too well to be caught by them, and as for Indians, they don't want him.

1

August 23. Cool, bright day, hinting Indian summer. Mr. Delaney has gone to the Smith Ranch, on the Tuolumne below Hetch-Hetchy Valley, thirty-five or forty miles from here, so I'll be alone for a week or more, — not really alone, for Carlo has come back. He was at a camp a few miles to the northwestward. He looked sheepish and ashamed when I asked him where he had been and why he had gone away without leave. He is now trying to get me to caress him and show signs of forgiveness. A wondrous wise dog. A great load is off my mind. I could not have left the mountains without him. He seems very glad to get back to me.

Rose and crimson sunset, and soon after the stars appeared the moon rose in most impressive majesty over the top of Mount Dana. I sauntered up the meadow in the white light. The jet-black tree-shadows were so wonderfully distinct and substantial looking, I often stepped high in crossing them, taking them for black charred logs.

August 24. Another charming day, warm and calm soon after sunrise, clouds only about .01, ⇀ faint, silky cirrus wisps, scarcely visible. Slight frost, Indian summerish, the mountains growing softer in outline and dreamy looking, their rough angles melted off, apparently. Sky at evening with fine, dark, subdued purple, almost like the evening purple of the San Joaquin plains in settled weather. The moon is now gazing over the summit of Dana. Glorious exhilarating air. I wonder if in all the world there is another mountain range of equal height blessed with weather so fine, and so openly kind and hospitable and approachable.

August 25. Cool as usual in the morning, quickly changing to the ordinary serene generous warmth and brightness. Toward evening the west wind was cool and sent us to the campfire. Of all Nature's flowery carpeted mountain halls none can be finer than this glacier meadow. Bees and butterflies seem as abundant as ever. The birds are still here, showing no sign of leaving for winter quarters though the frost must bring them to mind. For my part I should like to stay here all winter or all my life or even all eternity.

August 26. Frost this morning; all the meadow grass and some of the pine needles sparkling with irised crystals, — flowers of light. Large picturesque clouds, craggy like rocks, are piled on Mount Dana, reddish in color like the mountain itself; the sky for a few degrees around the horizon is pale purple, into which the pines dip their spires with fine effect. Spent the day as usual looking about me, watching the changing lights, the ripening autumn

3

colors of the grass, seeds, late-blooming gentians, asters, goldenrods; parting the meadow grass here and there and looking down into the underworld of mosses and liverworts; watching the busy ants and beetles and other small people at work and play like squirrels and bears in a forest; studying the formation of lakes and meadows, moraines, mountain sculpture; making small beginnings in these directions, charmed by the serene beauty of everything.

The day has been extra cloudy, though bright on the whole, for the clouds were brighter than common. Clouds about .15, which in Switzerland would be considered extra clear. Probably more free sunshine falls on this majestic range than on any other in the world I've ever seen or heard of. It has the brightest weather, brightest glacier-polished rocks, the greatest abundance of irised spray from its glorious waterfalls, the brightest forests of silver firs and silver pines, more starshine, moonshine, and perhaps more crystalshine than any other mountain chain, and its countless mirror lakes, having more light poured into them, glow and spangle most. And how glorious the shining after the short summer showers and after frosty nights when the morning sunbeams are pouring through the crystals on the grass and pine needles, and how ineffa-

4

bly spiritually fine is the morning-glow on the mountain-tops and the alpenglow of evening. Well may the Sierra be named, not the Snowy Range, but the Range of Light.

August 27. Clouds only .05, — mostly white and pink cumuli over the Hoffman spur towards evening, — frosty morning. Crystals grow in marvelous beauty and perfection of form these still nights, every one built as carefully as the grandest holiest temple, as if planned to endure forever.

Contemplating the lace-like fabric of streams outspread over the mountains, we are reminded that everything is flowing — going somewhere, animals and so-called lifeless rocks as well as water. Thus the snow flows fast or slow in grand beauty-making glaciers and avalanches; the air in majestic floods carrying minerals, plant leaves, seeds, spores, with streams of music and fragrance; water streams carrying rocks both in solution and in the form of mud particles, sand, pebbles, and boulders. Rocks flow from volcanoes like water from springs, and animals flock together and flow in currents modified by stepping, leaping, gliding, flying, swimming, etc. While the stars go streaming through space pulsed on and on forever like blood globules in Nature's warm heart.

August 28. The dawn a glorious song of

color. Sky absolutely cloudless. A fine crop of hoarfrost. Warm after ten o'clock. The gentians don't mind the first frost though their petals seem so delicate; they close every night as if going to sleep, and awake fresh as ever in the morning sun-glory. The grass is a shade browner since last week, but there are no nipped wilted plants of any sort as far as I have seen. Butterflies and the grand host of smaller flies are benumbed every night, but they hover and dance in the sunbeams over the meadows before noon with no apparent lack of playful, joyful life. Soon they must all fall like petals in an orchard, dry and wrinkled, not a wing of all the mighty host left to tingle the air. Nevertheless new myriads will arise in the spring, rejoicing, exulting, as if laughing cold death to scorn.

August 29. Clouds about .05, slight frost. Bland serene Indian summer weather. Have been gazing all day at the mountains, watching the changing lights. More and more plainly are they clothed with light as a garment, white tinged with pale purple, palest during the midday hours, richest in the morning and evening. Everything seems consciously peaceful, thoughtful, faithfully waiting God's will.

August 30. This day just like yesterday. A few clouds motionless and apparently with no

6

work to do beyond looking beautiful. Frost enough for crystal building, — glorious fields of ice-diamonds destined to last but a night. How lavish is Nature building, pulling down, creating, destroying, chasing every material particle from form to form, ever changing, ever beautiful.

Mr. Delaney arrived this morning. Felt not a trace of loneliness while he was gone. On the contrary, I never enjoyed grander company. The whole wilderness seems to be alive and familiar, full of humanity. The very stones seem talkative, sympathetic, brotherly. No wonder when we consider that we all have the same Father and Mother.

August 31. Clouds .05. Silky cirrus wisps and fringes so fine they almost escape notice. Frost enough for another crop of crystals on the meadows but none on the forests. The gentians, goldenrods, asters, etc., don't seem to feel it; neither petals nor leaves are touched though they seem so tender. Every day opens and closes like a flower, noiseless, effortless. Divine peace glows on all the majestic landscape like the silent enthusiastic joy that sometimes transfigures a noble human face.

September 1. Clouds .05 — motionless, of no particular color — ornaments with no hint of rain or snow in them. Day all calm — another grand throb of Nature's heart, ripening late flowers and seeds for next summer, full of life and the thoughts and plans of life to come, and full of ripe and ready death beautiful as life, telling divine wisdom and goodness and immortality. Have been up Mount Dana, making haste to see as much as I can now that the time of departure is drawing nigh. The views from the summit reach far and wide, eastward over the Mono Lake and Desert; mountains beyond mountains looking strangely barren and gray and bare like heaps of ashes dumped from the sky. The lake, eight or ten miles in diameter, shines like a burnished disk of silver, no trees about its gray, ashy, cindery shores. Looking westward, the glorious forests are seen sweeping over countless ridges and hills, girdling domes and subordinate mountains, fringing in long curving lines the dividing ridges, and filling every hollow where the glaciers have spread soil-beds however rocky or smooth. Looking northward and southward along the axis of the range, you see the glorious array of high mountains, crags and peaks and snow, the fountain-heads of rivers that are flowing west to the sea through the famous Golden Gate, and east to hot salt lakes and deserts to evaporate and hurry back into the sky. Innumerable lakes are shining like eyes beneath heavy rock brows, bare or tree fringed, or imbedded in black forests. Meadow openings in the woods seem as numerous as the lakes or perhaps more so. Far up the moraine-covered slopes and among crumbling rocks I found many delicate hardy plants, some of them still in flower. The best gains of this trip were the lessons of unity and interrelation of all the features of the landscape revealed in general views. The lakes and meadows are located just where the ancient glaciers bore heaviest at the foot of the steepest parts of their channels, and of course their longest diameters are approximately parallel with each other and with the belts of forests growing in long curving lines on the lateral and medial moraines, and in broad outspreading fields on the terminal beds deposited toward the end of the ice period when the glaciers were receding. The domes, ridges, and spurs also show the influence of glacial action in their forms, which approximately seem to be the forms of greatest strength with reference to the stress of oversweeping, past-sweeping, down-grinding ice-streams; survivals of the most resisting masses, or those most favorably situated. How interesting everything is! Every rock, mountain, stream, plant, lake, lawn, forest, garden, bird, beast, insect seems to call and invite us to come and learn something of its history and relationship. But shall the poor ignorant scholar be allowed to try the lessons they offer? It seems too great and good to be true. Soon I'll be going to the lowlands. The bread camp must soon be removed. If I had a few sacks of flour, an axe, and some matches, I would build a cabin of pine logs, pile up plenty of firewood about it and stay all winter to see the grand fertile snow-storms, watch the birds and animals that winter thus high, how they live, how the forests look snow-laden or buried, and how the avalanches look and sound on their way down the mountains. But now I'll have to go, for there is nothing to spare in the way of provisions. I'll surely be back, however, surely I'll be back. No other place has ever so overwhelmingly attracted me as this hospitable, Godful wilderness.

September 2. A grand, red, rosy, crimson day, — a perfect glory of a day. What it means I don't know. It is the first marked change from tranquil sunshine with purple mornings and evenings and still, white noons. There is nothing like a storm, however. The average cloudiness only about .08, and there is no sighing in the woods to betoken a big weather change. The sky was red in the

morning and evening, the color not diffused
like the ordinary purple glow, but loaded upon
separate well-defined clouds that remained
motionless, as if anchored around the jagged
mountain-fenced horizon. A deep-red cap,
bluffy around its sides, lingered a long time
on Mount Dana and Mount Gibbs, drooping
so low as to hide most of their bases, but leaving Dana's round summit free, which seemed
to float separate and alone over the big crimson
cloud. Mammoth Mountain, to the south of
Gibbs and Bloody Cañon, striped and spotted
with snow-banks and clumps of dwarf pine,
was also favored with a glorious crimson cap,
in the making of which there was no trace of
economy — a huge bossy pile colored with a
perfect passion of crimson that seemed important enough to be sent off to burn among the
stars in majestic independence. One is constantly reminded of the infinite lavishness and
fertility of Nature — inexhaustible abundance
amid what seems enormous waste. And yet
when we look into any of her operations that
lie within reach of our minds, we learn that
no particle of her material is wasted or worn
out. It is eternally flowing from use to use,
beauty to yet higher beauty; and we soon cease
to lament waste and death, and rather rejoice
and exult in the imperishable, unspendable

wealth of the universe, and faithfully watch and wait the reappearance of everything that melts and fades and dies about us, feeling sure that its next appearance will be better and more beautiful than the last.

I watched the growth of these red-lands of the sky as eagerly as if new mountain ranges were being built. Soon the group of snowy peaks in whose recesses lie the highest fountains of the Tuolumne, Merced, and North Fork of the San Joaquin were decorated with majestic colored clouds like those already described, but more complicated, to correspond with the grand fountain-heads of the rivers they overshadowed. The Sierra Cathedral, to the south of camp, was overshadowed like Sinai. Never before noticed so fine a union of rock and cloud in form and color and substance, drawing earth and sky together as one; and so human is it, every feature and tint of color goes to one's heart, and we shout, exulting in wild enthusiasm as if all the divine show were our own. More and more, in a place like this, we feel ourselves part of wild Nature, kin to everything. Spent most of the day high up on the north rim of the valley, commanding views of the clouds in all their red glory spreading their wonderful light over all the basin, while the rocks and trees and small Alpine plants at my feet seemed hushed and thoughtful, as if they also were conscious spectators of the glorious new cloud-world.

Here and there, as I plodded farther and higher, I came to small garden-patches and ferneries just where one would naturally decide that no plant-creature could possibly live. But, as in the region about the head of Mono Pass and the top of Dana, it was in the wildest, highest places that the most beautiful and tender and enthusiastic plant-people were found. Again and again, as I lingered over these charming plants, I said, How came you here? How do you live through the winter? Our roots, they explained, reach far down the joints of the summer-warmed rocks, and beneath our fine snow mantle killing frosts cannot reach us, while we sleep away the dark half of the year dreaming of spring.

Ever since I was allowed entrance into these mountains I have been looking for cassiope, said to be the most beautiful and best loved of the heathworts, but, strange to say, I have not yet found it. On my high mountain walks I keep muttering, "Cassiope, cassiope." This name, as Calvinists say, is driven in upon me, notwithstanding the glorious host of plants that come about me uncalled as soon as I show myself. Cassiope seems the highest name of

13

all the small mountain-heath people, and as if conscious of her worth, keeps out of my way. I must find her soon, if at all this year.

September 4. All the vast sky dome is clear, filled only with mellow Indian summer light. The pine and hemlock and fir cones are nearly ripe and are falling fast from morning to night, cut off and gathered by the busy squirrels. Almost all the plants have matured their seeds, their summer work done; and the summer crop of birds and deer will soon be able to follow their parents to the foothills and plains at the approach of winter, when the snow begins to fly.

September 5. No clouds. Weather cool, calm, bright as if no great thing was yet ready to be done. Have been sketching the North Tuolumne Church. The sunset gloriously colored.

September 6. Still another perfectly cloudless day, purple evening and morning, all the middle hours one mass of pure serene sunshine. Soon after sunrise the air grew warm, and there was no wind. One naturally halted to see what Nature intended to do. There is a suggestion of real Indian summer in the hushed brooding, faintly hazy weather. The yellow atmosphere, though thin, is still plainly of the same general character as that of eastern

Indian summer. The peculiar mellowness is perhaps in part caused by myriads of ripe spores adrift in the sky.

Mr. Delaney now keeps up a solemn talk about the need of getting away from these high mountains, telling sad stories of flocks that perished in storms that broke suddenly into the midst of fine innocent weather like this we are now enjoying. "In no case," said he, "will I venture to stay so high and far back in the mountains as we now are later than the middle of this month, no matter how warm and sunny it may be." He would move the flock slowly at first, a few miles a day until the Yosemite Creek basin was reached and crossed, then while lingering in the heavy pine woods should the weather threaten he could hurry down to the foothills, where the snow never falls deep enough to smother a sheep. Of course I am anxious to see as much of the wilderness as possible in the few days left me, and I say again, — May the good time come when I can stay as long as I like with plenty of bread, far and free from trampling flocks, though I may well be thankful for this generous foodful inspiring summer. Anyhow we never know where we must go nor what guides we are to get, — men, storms, guardian angels, or sheep. Perhaps almost everybody in the least natural is guarded more than he is ever aware of. All the wilderness seems to be full of tricks and plans to drive and draw us up into God's Light.

Have been busy planning, and baking bread for at least one more good wild excursion among the high peaks, and surely none, however hopefully aiming at fortune or fame, ever felt so gloriously happily excited by the outlook.

September 7. Left camp at daybreak and made direct for Cathedral Peak, intending to strike eastward and southward from that point among the peaks and ridges at the heads of the Tuolumne, Merced, and San Joaquin Rivers. Down through the pine woods I made my way, across the Tuolumne River and meadows, and up the heavily timbered slope forming the south boundary of the upper Tuolumne basin, along the east side of Cathedral Peak, and up to its topmost spire, which I reached at noon, having loitered by the way to study the fine trees — two-leaved pine, mountain pine, albicaulis pine, silver fir, and the most charming, most graceful of all the evergreens, the mountain hemlock. High, cool, late-flowering meadows also detained me, and lakelets and avalanche tracks and huge quarries of moraine rocks above the forests.

All the way up from the Big Meadows to the base of the Cathedral the ground is covered with moraine material, the left lateral moraine of the great glacier that must have completely filled this upper Tuolumne basin. Higher there are several small terminal moraines of residual glaciers shoved forward at right angles against the grand simple lateral of the main Tuolumne Glacier. A fine place to study mountain sculpture and soil making. The view from the Cathedral Spires is very fine and telling in every direction. Innumerable peaks, ridges, domes, meadows, lakes, and woods; the forests extending in long curving lines and broad fields wherever the glaciers have left soil for them to grow on, while the sides of the highest mountains show a straggling dwarf growth clinging to rifts in the rocks apparently independent of soil. The dark heath-like growth on the Cathedral roof I found to be dwarf snow-pressed albicaulis pine, about three or four feet high, but very old looking. Many of them are bearing cones, and the noisy Clarke crow is eating the seeds, using his long bill like a woodpecker in digging them out of the cones. A good many flowers are still in bloom about the base of the peak, and even on the roof among the little pines, especially a woody yellow-flowered eri-

ogonum and a handsome aster. The body of
the Cathedral is nearly square, and the roof
slopes are wonderfully regular and symmetri-
cal, the ridge trending northeast and southwest. This direction has apparently been
determined by structure joints in the granite.
The gable on the northeast end is magnificent
in size and simplicity, and at its base there is
a big snow-bank protected by the shadow of
the building. The front is adorned with many
pinnacles and a tall spire of curious work-
manship. Here too the joints in the rock are
seen to have played an important part in de-
termining their forms and size and general ar-
rangement. The Cathedral is said to be about
eleven thousand feet above the sea, but the
height of the building itself above the level
of the ridge it stands on is about fifteen hundred feet. A mile or so to the westward there
is a handsome lake, and the glacier-polished
granite about it is shining so brightly it is not
easy in some places to trace the line between
the rock and water, both shining alike. Of
this lake with its silvery basin and bits of
meadow and groves I have a fine view from
the spires; also of Lake Tenaya, Cloud's Rest
and the South Dome of Yosemite, Mount Starr
King, Mount Hoffman, the Merced peaks,
and the vast multitude of snowy fountain

18

peaks extending far north and south along the
axis of the range. No feature, however, of all
the noble landscape as seen from here seems
more wonderful than the Cathedral itself, a
temple displaying Nature's best masonry and
sermons in stones. How often I have gazed
at it from the tops of hills and ridges, and
through openings in the forests on my many
short excursions, devoutly wondering, admiring, longing! This I may say is the first time
I have been at church in California, led here
at last, every door graciously opened for the
poor lonely worshiper. In our best times everything turns into religion, all the world seems
a church and the mountains altars. And lo,
here at last in front of the Cathedral is blessed
cassiope, ringing her thousands of sweet-toned
bells, the sweetest church music I ever enjoyed. Listening, admiring, until late in the
afternoon I compelled myself to hasten away
eastward back of rough, sharp, spiry, splintery
peaks, all of them granite like the Cathedral,
sparkling with crystals — feldspar, quartz,
hornblende, mica, tourmaline. Had a rather
difficult walk and creep across an immense
snow and ice cliff which gradually increased
in steepness as I advanced until it was almost
impassable. Slipped on a dangerous place,
but managed to stop by digging my heels into

the thawing surface just on the brink of a yawning ice gulf. Camped beside a little pool and a group of crinkled dwarf pines; and as I sit by the fire trying to write notes the shallow pool seems fathomless with the infinite starry heavens in it, while the onlooking rocks and trees, tiny shrubs and daisies and sedges, brought forward in the fire-glow, seem full of thought as if about to speak aloud and tell all their wild stories. A marvelously impressive meeting in which every one has something worth while to tell. And beyond the fire-beams out in the solemn darkness, how impressive is the music of a choir of rills singing their way down from the snow to the river! And when we call to mind that thousands of these rejoicing rills are assembled in each one of the main streams, we wonder the less that our Sierra rivers are songful all the way to the sea.

About sundown saw a flock of dun grayish sparrows going to roost in crevices of a crag above the big snow-field. Charming little mountaineers! Found a species of sedge in flower within eight or ten feet of a snow-bank. Judging by the looks of the ground, it can hardly have been out in the sunshine much longer than a week, and it is likely to be buried again in fresh snow in a month or so, thus making a winter about ten months long, while spring, summer, and autumn are crowded and hurried into two months. How delightful it is to be alone here! How wild everything is — wild as the sky and as pure! Never shall I forget this big, divine day — the Cathedral and its thousands of cassiope bells, and the landscapes around them, and this camp in the gray crags above the woods, with its stars and streams and snow.

September 8. Day of climbing, scrambling, sliding on the peaks around the highest source of the Tuolumne and Merced. Climbed three of the most commanding of the mountains, whose names I don't know; crossed streams and huge beds of ice and snow more than I could keep count of. Neither could I keep count of the lakes scattered on tablelands and in the cirques of the peaks, and in chains in the cañons, linked together by the streams — a tremendously wild gray wilderness of hacked, shattered crags, ridges, and peaks, a few clouds drifting over and through the midst of them as if looking for work. In general views all the immense round landscape seems raw and lifeless as a quarry, yet the most charming flowers were found rejoicing in countless nooks and garden-like patches everywhere. I must have done three or four days' climbing work in this

21

one. Limbs perfectly tireless until near sundown, when I descended into the main upper Tuolumne valley at the foot of Mount Lyell, the camp still eight or ten miles distant. Going up through the pine woods past the Soda Springs Dome in the dark, where there is much fallen timber, and when all the excitement of seeing things was wanting, I was tired. Arrived at the main camp at nine o'clock, and soon was sleeping sound as death.

EARLY one bright morning in the middle of Indian summer, while the glacier meadows were still crisp with frost crystals, I set out from the foot of Mount Lyell, on my way down to Yosemite Valley, to replenish my exhausted store of bread and tea. I had spent the past summer, as many preceding ones, exploring the glaciers that lie on the head waters of the San Joaquin, Tuolumne, Merced, and Owen's Rivers; measuring and studying their movements, trends, crevasses, moraines, etc., and the part they had played during the period of their greater extension in the creation and development of the landscapes of this alpine wonderland. The time for this kind of work was nearly over for the year, and I began to look forward with delight to the approaching winter with its wondrous storms, when I would be warmly snow-bound in my Yosemite cabin with plenty of bread and books; but a tinge of regret came on when I considered that possibly I might not see this favorite region again until the next summer, excepting distant views from the heights about the Yosemite walls.

23

MOUNTAINEERING ESSAYS

To artists, few portions of the High Sierra are, strictly speaking, picturesque. The whole massive uplift of the range is one great picture, not clearly divisible into smaller ones; differing much in this respect from the older, and what may be called, riper mountains of the Coast Range. All the landscapes of the Sierra, as we have seen, were born again, remodeled from base to summit by the developing ice floods of the last glacial winter. But all these new landscapes were not brought forth simultaneously; some of the highest, where the ice lingered longest, are tens of centuries younger than those of the warmer regions below them. In general, the younger the mountain landscapes, — younger, I mean, with reference to the time of their emergence from the ice of the glacial period, — the less separable are they into artistic bits capable of being made into warm, sympathetic, lovable pictures with appreciable humanity in them.

Here, however, on the head waters of the Tuolumne, is a group of wild peaks on which the geologist may say that the sun has but just begun to shine, which is yet in a high degree picturesque, and in its main features so regular and evenly balanced as almost to appear conventional — one somber cluster of snow-laden peaks with gray, pine-fringed, granite bosses

24

braided around its base, the whole surging free into the sky from the head of a magnificent valley, whose lofty walls are beveled away on both sides so as to embrace it all without admitting anything not strictly belonging to it. The foreground was now aflame with autumn colors, brown and purple and gold, ripe in the mellow sunshine; contrasting brightly with the deep, cobalt blue of the sky, and the black and gray, and pure, spiritual white of the rocks and glaciers. Down through the midst, the young Tuolumne was seen pouring from its crystal fountains, now resting in glassy pools as if changing back again into ice, now leaping in white cascades as if turning to snow; gliding right and left between granite bosses, then sweeping on through the smooth, meadowy levels of the valley, swaying pensively from side to side with calm, stately gestures past dipping willows and sedges, and around groves of arrowy pine; and throughout its whole eventful course, whether flowing fast or slow, singing loud or low, ever filling the landscape with spiritual animation, and manifesting the grandeur of its sources in every movement and tone.

Pursuing my lonely way down the valley, I turned again and again to gaze on the glorious picture, throwing up my arms to inclose it as in

a frame. After long ages of growth in the darkness beneath the glaciers, through sunshine
and storms, it seemed now to be ready and
waiting for the elected artist, like yellow wheat
for the reaper; and I could not help wishing
that I might carry colors and brushes with me
on my travels, and learn to paint. In the mean
time I had to be content with photographs on
my mind and sketches in my notebooks. At
length, after I had rounded a precipitous headland that puts out from the west wall of the
valley, every peak vanished from sight, and I
pushed rapidly along the frozen meadows, over
the divide between the waters of the Merced
and Tuolumne, and down through the forests
that clothe the slopes of Cloud's Rest, arriving
in Yosemite in due time — which, with me, is
any time. And, strange to say, among the first
people I met here were two artists who, with
letters of introduction, were awaiting my return. They inquired whether in the course of
my explorations in the adjacent mountains I
had ever come upon a landscape suitable for a
large painting; whereupon I began a description of the one that had so lately excited my
admiration. Then, as I went on further and
further into details, their faces began to glow,
and I offered to guide them to it, while they
declared that they would gladly follow, far or

near, whithersoever I could spare the time to lead them.

Since storms might come breaking down through the fine weather at any time, burying the colors in snow, and cutting off the artists' retreat, I advised getting ready at once.

I led them out of the valley by the Vernal and Nevada Falls, thence over the main dividing ridge to the Big Tuolumne Meadows, by the old Mono Trail, and thence along the Upper Tuolumne River to its head. This was my companions' first excursion into the High Sierra, and as I was almost always alone in my mountaineering, the way that the fresh beauty was reflected in their faces made for me a novel and interesting study. They naturally were affected most of all by the colors — the intense azure of the sky, the purplish grays of the granite, the red and browns of dry meadows, and the translucent purple and crimson of huckleberry bogs; the flaming yellow of aspen groves, the silvery flashing of the streams, and the bright green and blue of the glacier lakes. But the general expression of the scenery — rocky and savage — seemed sadly disappointing; and as they threaded the forest from ridge to ridge, eagerly scanning the landscapes as they were unfolded, they said: "All this is huge and sublime, but we see nothing as yet at all available

27

for effective pictures. Art is long, and art is limited, you know; and here are foregrounds, middle-grounds, backgrounds, all alike; bare rock waves, woods, groves, diminutive flecks of meadow, and strips of glittering water." "Never mind," I replied, "only bide a wee, and I will show you something you will like."

At length, toward the end of the second day, the Sierra Crown began to come into view, and when we had fairly rounded the projecting headland before mentioned, the whole picture stood revealed in the flush of the alpenglow. Their enthusiasm was excited beyond bounds, and the more impulsive of the two, a young Scotchman, dashed ahead, shouting and gesticulating and tossing his arms in the air like a madman. Here, at last, was a typical alpine landscape.

After feasting a while on the view, I proceeded to make camp in a sheltered grove a little way back from the meadow, where pine boughs could be obtained for beds, and where there was plenty of dry wood for fires, while the artists ran here and there, along the river bends and up the sides of the cañon, choosing foregrounds for sketches. After dark, when our tea was made and a rousing fire had been built, we began to make our plans. They decided to remain several days, at the least, while I concluded to make an excursion in the mean time to the untouched summit of Ritter.

It was now about the middle of October, the springtime of snow-flowers. The first winter clouds had already bloomed, and the peaks were strewn with fresh crystals, without, however, affecting the climbing to any dangerous extent. And as the weather was still profoundly calm, and the distance to the foot of the mountain only a little more than a day, I felt that I was running no great risk of being storm-bound.

Mount Ritter is king of the mountains of the middle portion of the High Sierra, as Shasta of the north and Whitney of the south sections. Moreover, as far as I know, it had never been climbed. I had explored the adjacent wilderness summer after summer, but my studies thus far had never drawn me to the top of it. Its height above sea-level is about 13,300 feet, and it is fenced round by steeply inclined glaciers, and cañons of tremendous depth and ruggedness, which render it almost inaccessible. But difficulties of this kind only exhilarate the mountaineer.

Next morning, the artists went heartily to their work and I to mine. Former experiences had given good reason to know that passionate storms, invisible as yet, might be brooding in the calm sungold; therefore, before bidding farewell, I warned the artists not to be alarmed should I fail to appear before a week or ten days, and advised them, in case a snowstorm should set in, to keep up big fires and shelter themselves as best they could, and on no account to become frightened and attempt to seek their way back to Yosemite alone through the drifts.

My general plan was simply this: to scale the cañon wall, cross over to the eastern flank of the range, and then make my way southward to the northern spurs of Mount Ritter in compliance with the intervening topography; for to push on directly southward from camp through the innumerable peaks and pinnacles that adorn this portion of the axis of the range, however interesting, would take too much time, besides being extremely difficult and dangerous at this time of year.

All my first day was pure pleasure; simply mountaineering indulgence, crossing the dry pathways of the ancient glaciers, traeing happy streams, and learning the habits of the birds and marmots in the groves and rocks. Before I had gone a mile from camp, I came to the foot of a white cascade that beats its way down a rugged gorge in the cañon wall, from a height of about nine hundred feet, and pours its throbbing waters into the Tuolumne. I was acquainted with its fountains, which, fortunately, lay in my course. What a fine traveling companion it proved to be, what songs it sang, and how passionately it told the mountain's own joy! Gladly I climbed along its dashing border, absorbing its divine music, and bathing from time to time in waftings of irised spray. Climbing higher, higher, new beauty came streaming on the sight: painted meadows, late-blooming gardens, peaks of rare architecture, lakes here and there, shining like silver, and glimpses of the forested middle region and the yellow lowlands far in the west. Beyond the range I saw the so-called Mono Desert, lying dreamily silent in thick purple light — a desert of heavy sunglare beheld from a desert of ice-burnished granite. Here the waters divide, shouting in glorious enthusiasm, and falling eastward to vanish in the volcanic sands and dry sky of the Great Basin, or westward to the Great Valley of California, and thence through the Bay of San Francisco and the Golden Gate to the sea.

Passing a little way down over the summit until I had reached an elevation of about ten thousand feet, I pushed on southward toward a group of savage peaks that stand guard about Ritter on the north and west, groping my way, and dealing instinctively with every obstacle as it presented itself. Here a huge gorge would be found cutting across my path, along the dizzy edge of which I scrambled until some less precipitous point was discovered where I might safely venture to the bottom and then, selecting some feasible portion of the opposite wall, re-ascend with the same slow caution. Massive, flat-topped spurs alternate with the gorges, plunging abruptly from the shoulders of the snowy peaks, and planting their feet in the warm desert. These were everywhere marked and adorned with characteristic sculptures of the ancient glaciers that swept over this entire region like one vast ice wind, and the polished surfaces produced by the ponderous flood are still so perfectly preserved that in many places the sunlight reflected from them is about as trying to the eyes as sheets of snow.

God's glacial mills grind slowly, but they have been kept in motion long enough in California to grind sufficient soil for a glorious abundance of life, though most of the grist has been carried to the lowlands, leaving these high regions comparatively lean and bare; while the post-glacial agents of erosion have not yet furnished sufficient available food over the general surface for more than a few tufts of the hardiest plants, chiefly carices and eriogonæ. And it is interesting to learn in this connection that the sparseness and repressed character of the vegetation at this height is caused more by want of soil than by harshness of climate; for, here and there, in sheltered hollows (countersunk beneath the general surface) into which a few rods of well-ground moraine chips have been dumped, we find groves of spruce and pine thirty to forty feet high, trimmed around the edges with willow and huckleberry bushes, and oftentimes still further by an outer ring of tall grasses, bright with lupines, larkspurs, and showy columbines, suggesting a climate by no means repressingly severe. All the streams, too, and the pools at this elevation are furnished with little gardens wherever soil can be made to lie, which, though making scarce any show at a distance, constitute charming surprises to the appreciative observer. In these bits of leafiness a few birds find grateful homes. Having no acquaintance with man, they fear no ill, and flock curiously about the stranger, almost allowing themselves to be taken in the hand. In so wild and so beautiful a region was spent my first day, every sight and sound inspiring, leading one far out of himself, yet feeding and building up his individuality.

Now came the solemn, silent evening. Long, blue, spiky shadows crept out across the snow-fields, while a rosy glow, at first scarce discernible, gradually deepened and suffused every mountain-top, flushing the glaciers and the harsh crags above them. This was the alpenglow, to me one of the most impressive of all the terrestrial manifestations of God. At the touch of this divine light, the mountains seemed to kindle to a rapt, religious consciousness, and stood hushed and waiting like devout worshipers. Just before the alpenglow began to fade, two crimson clouds came streaming across the summit like wings of flame, rendering the sublime scene yet more impressive; then came darkness and the stars.

Icy Ritter was still miles away, but I could proceed no farther that night. I found a good camp-ground on the rim of a glacier basin about eleven thousand feet above the sea. A small lake nestles in the bottom of it, from which I got water for my tea, and a storm-beaten thicket near by furnished abundance of resiny firewood. Somber peaks, hacked and shattered, circled halfway around the horizon, wearing a savage aspect in the gloaming, and a waterfall chanted solemnly across the lake on its way down from the foot of a glacier. The fall and the lake and the glacier were almost equally bare; while the scraggy pines anchored in the rock-fissures were so dwarfed and shorn by storm-winds that you might walk over their tops. In tone and aspect the scene was one of

the most desolate I ever beheld. But the dark-
est scriptures of the mountains are illumined
with bright passages of love that never fail to
make themselves felt when one is alone.

I made my bed in a nook of the pine thicket,
where the branches were pressed and crinkled
overhead like a roof, and bent down around
the sides. These are the best bedchambers
the high mountains afford — snug as squirrel
nests, well-ventilated, full of spicy odors, and
with plenty of wind-played needles to sing one
asleep. I little expected company, but, creeping in through a low side door, I found five or
six birds nestling among the tassels. The night
wind began to blow soon after dark; at first
only a gentle breathing, but increasing toward
midnight to a rough gale that fell upon my
leafy roof in ragged surges like a cascade, bearing wild sounds from the crags overhead. The
waterfall sang in chorus, filling the old ice fountain with its solemn roar, and seeming to increase in power as the night advanced — fit
voice for such a landscape. I had to creep out
many times to the fire during the night, for it
was biting cold and I had no blankets. Gladly
I welcomed the morning star.

The dawn in the dry, wavering air of the
desert was glorious. Everything encouraged
my undertaking and betokened success. There

was no cloud in the sky, no storm tone in the wind. Breakfast of bread and tea was soon made. I fastened a hard, durable crust to my belt by way of provision, in case I should be compelled to pass a night on the mountain-top; then, securing the remainder of my little stock against wolves and wood rats, I set forth free and hopeful.

How glorious a greeting the sun gives the mountains! To behold this alone is worth the pains of any excursion a thousand times over. The highest peaks burned like islands in a sea of liquid shade. Then the lower peaks and spires caught the glow, and long lances of light, streaming through many a notch and pass, fell thick on the frozen meadows. The majestic form of Ritter was full in sight, and I pushed rapidly on over rounded rock bosses and pavements, my iron-shod shoes making a clanking sound, suddenly hushed now and then in rugs of bryanthus, and sedgy lake margins soft as moss. Here, too, in this so-called "land of desolation," I met cassiope, growing in fringes among the battered rocks. Her blossoms had faded long ago, but they were still clinging with happy memories to the evergreen sprays, and still so beautiful as to thrill every fiber of one's being. Winter and summer, you may hear her voice, the low, sweet melody of her purple bells.

36

No evangel among all the mountain plants speaks Nature's love more plainly than cassiope. Where she dwells, the redemption of the coldest solitude is complete. The very rocks and glaciers seem to feel her presence, and become imbued with her own fountain sweetness. All things were warming and awakening. Frozen rills began to flow, the marmots came out of their nests in boulder piles and climbed sunny rocks to bask, and the dun-headed sparrows were flitting about seeking their breakfasts. The lakes seen from every ridge-top were brilliantly rippled and spangled, shimmering like the thickets of the low dwarf pines. The rocks, too, seemed responsive to the vital heat — rock crystals and snow crystals thrilling alike. I strode on exhilarated, as if never more to feel fatigue, limbs moving of themselves, every sense unfolding like the thawing flowers, to take part in the new day harmony.

All along my course thus far, excepting when down in the cañons, the landscapes were mostly open to me, and expansive, at least on one side. On the left were the purple plains of Mono, reposing dreamily and warm; on the right, the near peaks springing keenly into the thin sky with more and more impressive sublimity. But these larger views were at length lost. Rugged spurs, and moraines, and huge, projecting buttresses began to shut me in. Every feature became more rigidly alpine, without, however, producing any chilling effect; for going to the mountains is like going home. We always find that the strangest objects in these fountain wilds are in some degree familiar, and we look upon them with a vague sense of having seen them before.

On the southern shore of a frozen lake, I encountered an extensive field of hard, granular snow, up which I scampered in fine tone, intending to follow it to its head, and cross the rocky spur against which it leans, hoping thus to come direct upon the base of the main Ritter peak. The surface was pitted with oval hollows, made by stones and drifted pine needles that had melted themselves into the mass by the radiation of absorbed sun-heat. These afforded good footholds, but the surface curved more and more steeply at the head, and the pits became shallower and less abundant, until I found myself in danger of being shed off like avalanching snow. I persisted, however, creeping on all fours, and shuffling up the smoothest places on my back, as I had often done on burnished granite, until, after slipping several times, I was compelled to retrace my course to the bottom, and made my way around the west end of the lake, and thence up to the sum-

mit of the divide between the head waters of
Rush Creek and the northernmost tributaries
of the San Joaquin.

Arriving on the summit of this dividing crest,
one of the most exciting pieces of pure wilderness was disclosed that I ever discovered in
all my mountaineering. There, immediately
in front, loomed the majestic mass of Mount
Ritter, with a glacier swooping down its face
nearly to my feet, then curving westward and
pouring its frozen flood into a dark blue lake,
whose shores were bound with precipices of
crystalline snow; while a deep chasm drawn
between the divide and the glacier separated
the massive picture from everything else. I
could see only the one sublime mountain, the
one glacier, the one lake; the whole veiled with
one blue shadow — rock, ice, and water close
together, without a single leaf or sign of life.
After gazing spellbound, I began instinctively
to scrutinize every notch and gorge and weathered buttress of the mountain, with reference
to making the ascent. The entire front above
the glacier appeared as one tremendous precipice, slightly receding at the top, and bristling
with spires and pinnacles set above one another
in formidable array. Massive lichen-stained
battlements stood forward here and there,
hacked at the top with angular notches, and

separated by frosty gullies and recesses that have been veiled in shadow ever since their creation; while to right and left, as far as I could see, were huge, crumbling buttresses, offering no hope to the climber. The head of the glacier sends up a few finger-like branches through narrow *couloirs;* but these seemed too steep and short to be available, especially as I had no axe with which to cut steps, and the numerous narrow-throated gullies down which stones and snow are avalanched seemed hopelessly steep, besides being interrupted by vertical cliffs; while the whole front was rendered still more terribly forbidding by the chill shadow and the gloomy blackness of the rocks.

Descending the divide in a hesitating mood, I picked my way across the yawning chasm at the foot, and climbed out upon the glacier. There were no meadows now to cheer with their brave colors, nor could I hear the dun-headed sparrows, whose cheery notes so often relieve the silence of our highest mountains. The only sounds were the gurgling of small rills down in the veins and crevasses of the glacier, and now and then the rattling report of falling stones, with the echoes they shot out into the crisp air.

I could not distinctly hope to reach the summit from this side, yet I moved on across the glacier as if driven by fate. Contending with myself, the season is too far spent, I said, and even should I be successful, I might be storm-bound on the mountain; and in the cloud darkness, with the cliffs and crevasses covered with snow, how could I escape? No; I must wait till next summer. I would only approach the mountain now, and inspect it, creep about its flanks, learn what I could of its history, holding myself ready to flee on the approach of the first storm cloud. But we little know until tried how much of the uncontrollable there is in us, urging over glaciers and torrents, and up perilous heights, let the judgment forbid as it may.

I succeeded in gaining the foot of the cliff on the eastern extremity of the glacier, and there discovered the mouth of a narrow avalanche gully, through which I began to climb, intending to follow it as far as possible, and at least obtain some fine wild views for my pains. Its general course is oblique to the plane of the mountain-face, and the metamorphic slates of which the mountain is built are cut by cleavage planes in such a way that they weather off in angular blocks, giving rise to irregular steps that greatly facilitate climbing on the sheer places. I thus made my way into a wilderness of crumbling spires and battlements, built together in bewildering combinations, and glazed in many places with a thin coating of ice, which I had to hammer off with stones. The situation was becoming gradually more perilous; but, having passed several dangerous spots, I dared not think of descending; for, so steep was the entire ascent, one would inevitably fall to the glacier in case a single misstep were made. Knowing, therefore, the tried danger beneath, I became all the more anxious concerning the developments to be made above, and began to be conscious of a vague foreboding of what actually befell; not that I was given to fear, but rather because my instincts, usually so positive and true, seemed vitiated in some way, and were leading me astray. At length, after attaining an elevation of about 12,800 feet, I found myself at the foot of a sheer drop in the bed of the avalanche channel I was tracing, which seemed absolutely to bar further progress. It was only about forty-five or fifty feet high, and somewhat roughened by fissures and projections; but these seemed so slight and insecure, as footholds, that I tried hard to avoid the precipice altogether, by scaling the wall of the channel on either side. But, though less steep, the walls were smoother than the obstructing rock, and repeated efforts only showed that I must either go right ahead or turn back. The tried dangers beneath seemed

even greater than that of the cliff in front;
therefore, after scanning its face again and
again, I began to scale it, picking my holds
with intense caution. After gaining a point
about halfway to the top, I was suddenly
brought to a dead stop, with arms outspread,
clinging close to the face of the rock, unable to
move hand or foot either up or down. My doom
appeared fixed. I *must* fall. There would be
a moment of bewilderment, and then a lifeless
rumble down the one general precipice to the
glacier below.

When this final danger flashed upon me, I
became nerve-shaken for the first time since
setting foot on the mountains, and my mind
seemed to fill with a stifling smoke. But this
terrible eclipse lasted only a moment, when life
blazed forth again with preternatural clear-
ness. I seemed suddenly to become possessed
of a new sense. The other self, bygone experiences, Instinct, or Guardian Angel, — call it
what you will, — came forward and assumed
control. Then my trembling muscles became
firm again, every rift and flaw in the rock was
seen as through a microscope, and my limbs
moved with a positiveness and precision with
which I seemed to have nothing at all to do.
Had I been borne aloft upon wings, my deliv-
erance could not have been more complete.

Above this memorable spot, the face of the mountain is still more savagely hacked and torn. It is a maze of yawning chasms and gullies, in the angles of which rise beetling crags and piles of detached boulders that seem to have been gotten ready to be launched below. But the strange influx of strength I had received seemed inexhaustible. I found a way without effort, and soon stood upon the topmost crag in the blessed light.

How truly glorious the landscape circled around this noble summit! — giant mountains, valleys innumerable, glaciers and meadows, rivers and lakes, with the wide blue sky bent tenderly over them all. But in my first hour of freedom from that terrible shadow, the sunlight in which I was laving seemed all in all.

Looking southward along the axis of the range, the eye is first caught by a row of exceedingly sharp and slender spires, which rise openly to a height of about a thousand feet, above a series of short, residual glaciers that lean back against their bases; their fantastic sculpture and the unrelieved sharpness with which they spring out of the ice rendering them peculiarly wild and striking. These are "The Minarets." Beyond them you behold a sublime wilderness of mountains, their snowy summits towering together in crowded abundance,

44

peak beyond peak, swelling higher, higher, as they sweep on southward, until the culminating point of the range is reached on Mount Whitney, near the head of the Kern River, at an elevation of nearly 14,700 feet above the level of the sea.

Westward, the general flank of the range is seen flowing sublimely away from the sharp summits, in smooth undulations; a sea of huge gray granite waves dotted with lakes and meadows, and fluted with stupendous cañons that grow steadily deeper as they recede in the distance. Below this gray region lies the dark forest zone, broken here and there by upswelling ridges and domes; and yet beyond lies a yellow, hazy belt, marking the broad plain of the San Joaquin, bounded on its farther side by the blue mountains of the coast.

Turning now to the northward, there in the immediate foreground is the glorious Sierra Crown, with Cathedral Peak, a temple of marvelous architecture, a few degrees to the left of it; the gray, massive form of Mammoth Mountain to the right; while Mounts Ord, Gibbs, Dana, Conness, Tower Peak, Castle Peak, Silver Mountain, and a host of noble companions, as yet nameless, make a sublime show along the axis of the range.

Eastward, the whole region seems a land of

desolation covered with beautiful light. The torrid volcanic basin of Mono, with its one bare lake fourteen miles long; Owen's Valley and the broad lava tableland at its head, dotted with craters, and the massive Inyo Range, rivaling even the Sierra in height; these are spread, map-like, beneath you, with countless ranges beyond, passing and overlapping one another and fading on the glowing horizon.

At a distance of less than three thousand feet below the summit of Mount Ritter you may find tributaries of the San Joaquin and Owen's Rivers, bursting forth from the ice and snow of the glaciers that load its flanks; while a little to the north of here are found the highest affluents of the Tuolumne and Merced. Thus, the fountains of four of the principal rivers of California are within a radius of four or five miles.

Lakes are seen gleaming in all sorts of places, — round, or oval, or square, like very mirrors; others narrow and sinuous, drawn close around the peaks like silver zones, the highest reflecting only rocks, snow, and the sky. But neither these nor the glaciers, nor the bits of brown meadow and moorland that occur here and there, are large enough to make any marked impression upon the mighty wilderness of mountains. The eye, rejoicing in its freedom, roves about the vast expanse, yet returns again and again to the fountain peaks. Perhaps some one of the multitude excites special attention, some gigantic castle with turret and battlement, or some Gothic cathedral more abundantly spired than Milan's. But, generally, when looking for the first time from an all-embracing standpoint like this, the inexperienced observer is oppressed by the incomprehensible grandeur, variety, and abundance of the mountains rising shoulder to shoulder beyond the reach of vision; and it is only after they have been studied one by one, long and lovingly, that their far-reaching harmonies become manifest. Then, penetrate the wilderness where you may, the main telling features, to which all the surrounding topography is subordinate, are quickly perceived, and the most complicated clusters of peaks stand revealed harmoniously correlated and fashioned like works of art — eloquent monuments of the ancient ice rivers that brought them into relief from the general mass of the range. The cañons, too, some of them a mile deep, mazing wildly through the mighty host of mountains, however lawless and ungovernable at first sight they appear, are at length recognized as the necessary effects of causes which followed each other in harmonious sequence—Nature's poems carved on tables of stone — simplest and most emphatic of her glacial compositions.

Could we have been here to observe during the glacial period, we should have overlooked a wrinkled ocean of ice as continuous as that now covering the landscapes of Greenland; filling every valley and cañon with only the tops of the fountain peaks rising darkly above the rock-encumbered ice waves like islets in a stormy sea — those islets the only hints of the glorious landscapes now smiling in the sun. Standing here in the deep, brooding silence all the wilderness seems motionless, as if the work of creation were done. But in the midst of this outer steadfastness we know there is incessant motion and change. Ever and anon, avalanches are falling from yonder peaks. These cliff-bound glaciers, seemingly wedged and immovable, are flowing like water and grinding the rocks beneath them. The lakes are lapping their granite shores and wearing them away, and every one of these rills and young rivers is fretting the air into music, and carrying the mountains to the plains. Here are the roots of all the life of the valleys, and here more simply than elsewhere is the eternal flux of Nature manifested. Ice changing to water, lakes to meadows, and mountains to plains. And while we thus contemplate Nature's methods of land-

48

scape creation, and, reading the records she has carved on the rocks, reconstruct, however imperfectly, the landscapes of the past, we also learn that as these we now behold have succeeded those of the pre-glacial age, so they in turn are withering and vanishing to be succeeded by others yet unborn.

But in the midst of these fine lessons and landscapes, I had to remember that the sun was wheeling far to the west, while a new way down the mountain had to be discovered to some point on the timber line where I could have a fire; for I had not even burdened myself with a coat. I first scanned the western spurs, hoping some way might appear through which I might reach the northern glacier, and cross its snout, or pass around the lake into which it flows, and thus strike my morning track. This route was soon sufficiently unfolded to show that, if it were practicable at all, it would require so much time that reaching camp that night would be out of the question. I therefore scrambled back eastward, and descended the southern slopes obliquely at the same time. Here the crags seemed less formidable, and the head of a glacier that flows northeast came in sight, which I determined to follow as far as possible, hoping thus to make my way to the foot of the peak on the east side, and thence

49

across the intervening cañons and ridges to camp.

The inclination of the glacier is quite moderate at the head, and, as the sun had softened the *névé*, I made safe and rapid progress, running and sliding, and keeping up a sharp outlook for crevasses. About half a mile from the head, there is an ice cascade, where the glacier pours over a sharp declivity and is shattered into massive blocks separated by deep, blue fissures. To thread my way through the slippery mazes of this crevassed portion seemed impossible, and I endeavored to avoid it by climbing off to the shoulder of the mountain. But the slopes rapidly steepened and at length fell away in sheer precipices, compelling a return to the ice. Fortunately, the day had been warm enough to loosen the ice crystals so as to admit of hollows being dug in the rotten portions of the blocks, thus enabling me to pick my way with far less difficulty than I had anticipated. Continuing down over the snout, and along the left lateral moraine, was only a confident saunter, showing that the ascent of the mountain by way of this glacier is easy, provided one is armed with an axe to cut steps here and there.

The lower end of the glacier was beautifully waved and barred by the outcropping edges of the bedded ice layers which represent the annual snowfalls, and to some extent the irregularities of structure caused by the weathering of the walls of crevasses, and by separate snowfalls which have been followed by rain, hail, thawing and freezing, etc. Small rills were gliding and swirling over the melting surface with a smooth, oily appearance, in channels of pure ice — their quick, compliant movements contrasting most impressively with the rigid, invisible flow of the glacier itself, on whose back they all were riding.

Night drew near before I reached the eastern base of the mountain, and my camp lay many a rugged mile to the north; but ultimate success was assured. It was now only a matter of endurance and ordinary mountain-craft. The sunset was, if possible, yet more beautiful than that of the day before. The Mono landscape seemed to be fairly saturated with warm, purple light. The peaks marshaled along the summit were in shadow, but through every notch and pass streamed vivid sunfire, soothing and irradiating their rough, black angles, while companies of small, luminous clouds hovered above them like very angels of light.

Darkness came on, but I found my way by the trends of the cañons and the peaks projected against the sky. All excitement died with the light, and then I was weary. But the joyful sound of the waterfall across the lake was heard at last, and soon the stars were seen reflected in the lake itself. Taking my bearings from these, I discovered the little pine thicket in which my nest was, and then I had a rest such as only a tired mountaineer may enjoy. After lying loose and lost for a while, I made a sunrise fire, went down to the lake, dashed water on my head, and dipped a cupful for tea. The revival brought about by bread and tea was as complete as the exhaustion from excessive enjoyment and toil. Then I crept beneath the pine tassels to bed. The wind was frosty and the fire burned low, but my sleep was none the less sound, and the evening constellations had swept far to the west before I awoke.

After thawing and resting in the morning sunshine, I sauntered home, — that is, back to the Tuolumne camp, — bearing away toward a cluster of peaks that hold the fountain snows of one of the north tributaries of Rush Creek. Here I discovered a group of beautiful glacier lakes, nestled together in a grand amphitheater. Toward evening, I crossed the divide separating the Mono waters from those of the Tuolumne, and entered the glacier basin that now holds the fountain snows of the stream that forms the upper Tuolumne cascades. This stream I traced down through its many dells and gorges, meadows and bogs, reaching the brink of the main Tuolumne at dusk.

A loud whoop for the artists was answered again and again. Their camp-fire came in sight, and half an hour afterward I was with them. They seemed unreasonably glad to see me. I had been absent only three days; nevertheless, though the weather was fine, they had already been weighing chances as to whether I would ever return, and trying to decide whether they should wait longer or begin to seek their way back to the lowlands. Now their curious troubles were over. They packed their precious sketches, and next morning we set out homeward bound, and in two days entered the Yosemite Valley from the north by way of Indian Cañon.

PRAYERS IN HIGHER MOUNTAIN TEMPLES, OR
A GEOLOGIST'S WINTER WALK[1]

AFTER reaching Turlock, I sped afoot over the stubble fields and through miles of brown hemizonia and purple erigeron, to Hopeton, conscious of little more than that the town was behind and beneath me, and the mountains above and before me; on through the oaks and chaparral of the foothills to Coulterville; and then ascended the first great mountain step upon which grows the sugar pine. Here I slackened pace, for I drank the spicy, resiny wind, and beneath the arms of this noble tree I felt that I was safely home. Never did pine trees seem so dear. How sweet was their breath and their song, and how grandly they winnowed the sky! I tingled my fingers among their tassels, and rustled my feet among their brown needles and burrs, and was exhilarated and joyful beyond all I can write.

When I reached Yosemite, all the rocks seemed talkative, and more telling and lovable than ever. They are dear friends, and seemed to have warm blood gushing through their

[1] An excerpt from a letter to a friend, written in 1873. [Editor.]

55

granite flesh; and I love them with a love inten-
sified by long and close companionship. After
I had bathed in the bright river, sauntered over
the meadows, conversed with the domes, and
played with the pines, I still felt blurred and
weary, as if tainted in some way with the sky
of your streets. I determined, therefore, to
run out for a while to say my prayers in the
higher mountain temples. "The days are sunful," I said, "and, though now winter, no
great danger need be encountered, and no
sudden storm will block my return, if I am
watchful."

The morning after this decision, I started
up the cañon of Tenaya, caring little about
the quantity of bread I carried; for, I thought,
a fast and a storm and a difficult cañon were
just the medicine I needed. When I passed
Mirror Lake, I scarcely noticed it, for I was
absorbed in the great Tissiack — her crown a
mile away in the hushed azure; her purple
granite drapery flowing in soft and graceful
folds down to my feet, embroidered gloriously
around with deep, shadowy forest. I have
gazed on Tissiack a thousand times — in days
of solemn storms, and when her form shone
divine with the jewelry of winter, or was veiled
in living clouds; and I have heard her voice of
winds, and snowy, tuneful waters when floods

56

were falling; yet never did her soul reveal itself more impressively than now. I hung about her skirts, lingering timidly, until the higher mountains and glaciers compelled me to push up the cañon.

This cañon is accessible only to mountaineers, and I was anxious to carry my barometer and clinometer through it, to obtain sections and altitudes, so I chose it as the most attractive highway. After I had passed the tall groves that stretch a mile above Mirror Lake, and scrambled around the Tenaya Fall, which is just at the head of the lake groves, I crept through the dense and spiny chaparral that plushes the roots of the mountains here for miles in warm green, and was ascending a precipitous rock-front, smoothed by glacial action, when I suddenly fell — for the first time since I touched foot to Sierra rocks. After several somersaults, I became insensible from the shock, and when consciousness returned I found myself wedged among short, stiff bushes, trembling as if cold, not injured in the slightest.

Judging by the sun, I could not have been insensible very long; probably not a minute, possibly an hour; and I could not remember what made me fall, or where I had fallen from; but I saw that if I had rolled a little further, my mountain-climbing would have been finished, for just beyond the bushes the cañon wall steepened and I might have fallen to the bottom. "There," said I, addressing my feet, to whose separate skill I had learned to trust night and day on any mountain, "that is what you get by intercourse with stupid town stairs, and dead pavements." I felt degraded and worthless. I had not yet reached the most difficult portion of the cañon, but I determined to guide my humbled body over the most nerve-trying places I could find; for I was now awake, and felt confident that the last of the town fog had been shaken from both head and feet.

I camped at the mouth of a narrow gorge which is cut into the bottom of the main cañon, determined to take earnest exercise next day. No plushy boughs did my ill-behaved bones enjoy that night, nor did my bumped head get a spicy cedar plume pillow mixed with flowers. I slept on a naked boulder, and when I awoke all my nervous trembling was gone.

The gorged portion of the cañon, in which I spent all the next day, is about a mile and a half in length; and I passed the time in tracing the action of the forces that determined this peculiar bottom gorge, which is an abrupt, ragged-walled, narrow-throated cañon, formed in the bottom of the wide-mouthed, smooth, and beveled main cañon. I will not stop now to tell you more; some day you may see it, like a shadowy line, from Cloud's Rest. In high water, the stream occupies all the bottom of the gorge, surging and chafing in glorious power from wall to wall. But the sound of the grinding was low as I entered the gorge, scarcely hoping to be able to pass through its entire length. By cool efforts, along glassy, ice-worn slopes, I reached the upper end in a little over a day, but was compelled to pass the second night in the gorge, and in the moonlight I wrote you this short pencil-letter in my notebook: —

The moon is looking down into the cañon, and how marvelously the great rocks kindle to her light! Every dome, and brow, and swelling boss touched by her white rays, glows as if lighted with snow. I am now only a mile from last night's camp; and have been climbing and sketching all day in this difficult but instructive gorge. It is formed in the bottom of the main cañon, among the roots of Cloud's Rest. It begins at the filled-up lake-basin where I camped last night, and ends a few hundred yards above, in another basin of the same kind. The walls everywhere are craggy and vertical, and in some places they overlean. It is only from twenty to sixty feet wide, and not, though black and broken enough, the thin, crooked mouth of some mysterious abyss; but it was eroded, for in many places I saw its solid, seamless floor.

I am sitting on a big stone, against which the stream divides, and goes brawling by in rapids on both sides; half of my rock is white in the light, half in shadow. As I look from the opening jaws of this shadowy gorge, South Dome is immediately in front — high in the stars, her face turned from the moon, with the rest of her body gloriously muffled in waved folds of granite. On the left, sculptured from the main Cloud's Rest ridge, are three magnificent rocks, sisters of the great South Dome. On the right is the massive, moonlit front of Mount Watkins, and between, low down in the furthest distance, is Sentinel Dome, girdled and darkened with forest. In the near foreground Tenaya Creek is singing against boulders that are white with snow and moonbeams. Now look back twenty yards, and you will see a waterfall fair as a spirit; the moonlight just touches it, bringing it into relief against a dark background of shadow. A little to the left, and a dozen steps this side of the fall, a flickering light marks my camp — and a precious camp it is. A huge, glacier-polished slab, falling from the smooth, glossy flank of Cloud's Rest, happened to settle on edge against the wall of the gorge. I did not know that this slab was glacier-polished until I lighted my fire. Judge of my delight. I think it was sent here by an earthquake. It is about twelve feet square. I wish I could take it home[1] for a hearthstone. Beneath this slab is the only place in this torrent-swept gorge where I could find sand sufficient for a bed.

I expected to sleep on the boulders, for I spent most of the afternoon on the slippery wall of the cañon, endeavoring to get around this difficult part

[1] Muir at this time was making Yosemite Valley his home. [Editor.]

of the gorge, and was compelled to hasten down here for water before dark. I shall sleep soundly on this sand; half of it is mica. Here, wonderful to behold, are a few green stems of prickly rubus, and a tiny grass. They are here to meet us. Ay, even here in this darksome gorge, "frightened and tormented" with raging torrents and choking avalanches of snow. Can it be? As if rubus and the grass leaf were not enough of God's tender prattle words of love, which we so much need in these mighty temples of power, yonder in the "benmost bore" are two blessed adiantums. Listen to them! How wholly infused with God is this one big word of love that we call the world! Good-night. Do you see the fire-glow on my ice-smoothed slab, and on my two ferns and the rubus and grass panicles? And do you hear how sweet a sleep-song the fall and cascades are singing?

The water-ground chips and knots that I found fastened between the rocks kept my fire alive all through the night. Next morning I rose nerved and ready for another day of sketching and noting, and any form of climbing. I escaped from the gorge about noon, after accomplishing some of the most delicate feats of mountaineering I ever attempted; and here the cañon is all broadly open again — the floor luxuriantly forested with pine, and spruce, and silver fir, and brown-trunked librocedrus. The walls rise in Yosemite forms, and Tenaya Creek comes down seven hundred feet in a white brush of foam. This is a little Yosemite valley. It is about two thousand feet above the level of the main Yosemite, and about twenty-four hundred below Lake Tenaya.

I found the lake frozen, and the ice was so clear and unruffled that the surrounding mountains and the groves that look down upon it were reflected almost as perfectly as I ever beheld them in the calm evening mirrors of summer. At a little distance, it was difficult to believe the lake frozen at all; and when I walked out on it, cautiously stamping at short intervals to test the strength of the ice, I seemed to walk mysteriously, without adequate faith, on the surface of the water. The ice was so transparent that I could see through it the beautifully wave-rippled, sandy bottom, and the scales of mica glinting back the down-pouring light. When I knelt down with my face close to the ice, through which the sunbeams were pouring, I was delighted to discover myriads of Tyndall's six-rayed water flowers, magnificently colored.

A grand old mountain mansion is this Tenaya region! In the glacier period it was a *mer de glace*, far grander than the *mer de glace* of Switzerland, which is only about half a mile broad. The Tenaya *mer de glace* was not less than two miles broad, late in the glacier epoch,

62

when all the principal dividing crests were
bare; and its depth was not less than fifteen
hundred feet. Ice-streams from Mounts Lyell
and Dana, and all the mountains between, and
from the nearer Cathedral Peak, flowed hither,
welded into one, and worked together. After
eroding this Tenaya Lake basin, and all the
splendidly sculptured rocks and mountains
that surround and adorn it, and the great
Tenaya Cañon, with its wealth of all that
makes mountains sublime, they were welded
with the vast South, Lyell, and Illilouette
glaciers on one side, and with those of Hoffman
on the other — thus forming a portion of a yet
grander *mer de glace* in Yosemite Valley.

I reached the Tenaya Cañon, on my way
home, by coming in from the northeast, ram-
bling down over the shoulders of Mount Watkins, touching bottom a mile above Mirror
Lake. From thence home was but a saunter
in the moonlight.

After resting one day, and the weather continuing calm, I ran up over the left shoulder of
South Dome and down in front of its grand
split face to make some measurements, completed my work, climbed to the right shoulder,
struck off along the ridge for Cloud's Rest, and
reached the topmost heave of her sunny wave
in ample time to see the sunset.

Cloud's Rest is a thousand feet higher than Tissiack. It is a wavelike crest upon a ridge, which begins at Yosemite with Tissiack, and runs continuously eastward to the thicket of peaks and crests around Lake Tenaya. This lofty granite wall is bent this way and that by the restless and weariless action of glaciers just as if it had been made of dough. But the grand circumference of mountains and forests are coming from far and near, densing into one close assemblage; for the sun, their god and father, with love ineffable, is glowing a sunset farewell. Not one of all the assembled rocks or trees seemed remote. How impressively their faces shone with responsive love!

I ran home in the moonlight with firm strides; for the sun-love made me strong. Down through the junipers; down through the firs; now in jet shadows, now in white light; over sandy moraines and bare, clanking rocks; past the huge ghost of South Dome rising weird through the firs; past the glorious fall of Nevada, the groves of Illilouette; through the pines of the valley; beneath the bright crystal sky blazing with stars. All of this mountain wealth in one day! — one of the rich ripe days that enlarge one's life; so much of the sun upon one side of it, so much of the moon and stars on the other.

A PERILOUS NIGHT ON SHASTA'S SUMMIT

TOWARD the end of summer, after a light, open winter, one may reach the summit of Mount Shasta without passing over much snow, by keeping on the crest of a long narrow ridge, mostly bare, that extends from near the camp-ground at the timber-line. But on my first excursion to the summit the whole mountain, down to its low swelling base, was smoothly laden with loose fresh snow, presenting a most glorious mass of winter mountain scenery, in the midst of which I scrambled and reveled or lay snugly snowbound, enjoying the fertile clouds and the snow-bloom in all their growing, drifting grandeur.

I had walked from Redding, sauntering leisurely from station to station along the old Oregon stage-road, the better to see the rocks and plants, birds and people, by the way, tracing the rushing Sacramento to its fountains around icy Shasta. The first rains had fallen on the lowlands, and the first snows on the mountains, and everything was fresh and bracing, while an abundance of balmy sunshine filled all the noonday hours. It was the

65

calm afterglow that usually succeeds the first storm of the winter. I met many of the birds that had reared their young and spent their summer in the Shasta woods and chaparral. They were then on their way south to their winter homes, leading their young full-fledged and about as large and strong as the parents. Squirrels, dry and elastic after the storms, were busy about their stores of pine nuts, and the latest goldenrods were still in bloom, though it was now past the middle of October. The grand color glow — the autumnal jubilee of ripe leaves — was past prime, but, freshened by the rain, was still making a fine show along the banks of the river and in the ravines and the dells of the smaller streams.

At the salmon-hatching establishment on the McCloud River I halted a week to examine the limestone belt, grandly developed there, to learn what I could of the inhabitants of the river and its banks, and to give time for the fresh snow that I knew had fallen on the mountain to settle somewhat, with a view to making the ascent. A pedestrian on these mountain roads, especially so late in the year, is sure to excite curiosity, and many were the interrogations concerning my ramble. When I said that I was simply taking a walk, and that icy Shasta was my mark, I was invariably admonished that I had come on a dangerous quest. The time was far too late, the snow was too loose and deep to climb, and I should be lost in drifts and slides. When I hinted that new snow was beautiful and storms not so bad as they were called, my advisers shook their heads in token of superior knowledge and declared the ascent of "Shasta Butte" through loose snow impossible. Nevertheless, before noon of the second of November I was in the frosty azure of the utmost summit.

When I arrived at Sisson's everything was quiet. The last of the summer visitors had flitted long before, and the deer and bears also were beginning to seek their winter homes. My barometer and the sighing winds and filmy, half-transparent clouds that dimmed the sunshine gave notice of the approach of another storm, and I was in haste to be off and get myself established somewhere in the midst of it, whether the summit was to be attained or not. Sisson, who is a mountaineer, speedily fitted me out for storm or calm as only a mountaineer could, with warm blankets and a week's provisions so generous in quantity and kind that they easily might have been made to last a month in case of my being closely snowbound. Well I knew the weariness of snow-climbing, and the frosts, and the dangers of mountaineering so late in the year; therefore I could not ask a guide to go with me, even had one been willing. All I wanted was to have blankets and provisions deposited as far up in the timber as the snow would permit a pack-animal to go. There I could build a storm nest and lie warm, and make raids up and around the mountain in accordance with the weather.

Setting out on the afternoon of November first, with Jerome Fay, mountaineer and guide, in charge of the animals, I was soon plodding wearily upward through the muffled winter woods, the snow of course growing steadily deeper and looser, so that we had to break a trail. The animals began to get discouraged, and after night and darkness came on they became entangled in a bed of rough lava, where, breaking through four or five feet of mealy snow, their feet were caught between angular boulders. Here they were in danger of being lost, but after we had removed packs and saddles and assisted their efforts with ropes, they all escaped to the side of a ridge about a thousand feet below the timber-line.

To go farther was out of the question, so we were compelled to camp as best we could. A pitch-pine fire speedily changed the temperature and shed a blaze of light on the wild lava-slope and the straggling storm-bent pines around us. Melted snow answered for coffee, and we had plenty of venison to roast. Toward midnight I rolled myself in my blankets, slept an hour and a half, arose and ate more venison, tied two days' provisions to my belt, and set out for the summit, hoping to reach it ere the coming storm should fall. Jerome accompanied me a little distance above camp and indicated the way as well as he could in the darkness. He seemed loath to leave me, but, being reassured that I was at home and required no care, he bade me good-bye and returned to camp, ready to lead his animals down the mountain at daybreak.

After I was above the dwarf pines, it was fine practice pushing up the broad unbroken slopes of snow, alone in the solemn silence of the night. Half the sky was clouded; in the other half the stars sparkled icily in the keen, frosty air; while everywhere the glorious wealth of snow fell away from the summit of the cone in flowing folds, more extensive and continuous than any I had ever seen before. When day dawned the clouds were crawling slowly and becoming more massive, but gave no intimation of immediate danger, and I pushed on faithfully, though holding myself well in hand, ready to return to the timber; for it was easy to see that the storm was not far off. The mountain rises ten thousand feet above the general level of the country, in blank exposure to the deep upper currents of the sky, and no labyrinth of peaks and cañons I had ever been in seemed to me so dangerous as these immense slopes, bare against the sky.

The frost was intense, and drifting snow-dust made breathing at times rather difficult. The snow was as dry as meal, and the finer particles drifted freely, rising high in the air, while the larger portions of the crystals rolled like sand. I frequently sank to my armpits between buried blocks of loose lava, but generally only to my knees. When tired with walking I still wallowed slowly upward on all fours. The steepness of the slope — thirty-five degrees in some places — made any kind of progress fatiguing, while small avalanches were being constantly set in motion in the steepest places. But the bracing air and the sublime beauty of the snowy expanse thrilled every nerve and made absolute exhaustion impossible. I seemed to be walking and wallowing in a cloud; but, holding steadily onward, by half-past ten o'clock I had gained the highest summit.

I held my commanding foothold in the sky for two hours, gazing on the glorious landscapes spread maplike around the immense horizon, and tracing the outlines of the ancient lava-streams extending far into the surrounding plains, and the pathways of vanished glaciers of which Shasta had been the center. But, as I had left my coat in camp for the sake of having my limbs free in climbing, I soon was cold. The wind increased in violence, raising the snow in magnificent drifts that were drawn out in the form of wavering banners glowing in the sun. Toward the end of my stay a succession of small clouds struck against the summit rocks like drifting icebergs, darkening the air as they passed, and producing a chill as definite and sudden as if ice-water had been dashed in my face. This is the kind of cloud in which snow-flowers grow, and I turned and fled.

Finding that I was not closely pursued, I ventured to take time on the way down for a visit to the head of the Whitney Glacier and the "Crater Butte." After I reached the end of the main summit ridge the descent was but little more than one continuous soft, mealy, muffled slide, most luxurious and rapid, though the hissing, swishing speed attained was obscured in great part by flying snow-dust — a marked contrast to the boring seal-wallowing upward struggle. I reached camp about an hour before dusk, hollowed a strip of loose ground in the lee of a large block of red lava, where firewood was abundant, rolled myself in my blankets, and went to sleep.

Next morning, having slept little the night before the ascent and being weary with climbing after the excitement was over, I slept late. Then, awaking suddenly, my eyes opened on one of the most beautiful and sublime scenes I ever enjoyed. A boundless wilderness of storm-clouds of different degrees of ripeness were congregated over all the lower landscape for thousands of square miles, colored gray, and purple, and pearl, and deep-glowing white, amid which I seemed to be floating; while the great white cone of the mountain above was all aglow in the free, blazing sunshine. It seemed not so much an ocean as a *land* of clouds — undulating hill and dale, smooth purple plains, and silvery mountains of cumuli, range over range, diversified with peak and dome and hollow fully brought out in light and shade.

I gazed enchanted, but cold gray masses, drifting like dust on a wind-swept plain, began to shut out the light, forerunners of the coming storm I had been so anxiously watching. I made haste to gather as much wood as possible, snugging it as a shelter around my bed. The storm side of my blankets was fastened down with stakes to reduce as much as possible the sifting-in of drift and the danger of being blown away. The precious bread-sack was placed safely as a pillow, and when at length the first flakes fell I was exultingly ready to welcome them. Most of my firewood was more than half rosin and would blaze in the face of the fiercest drifting; the winds could not demolish my bed, and my bread could be made to last indefinitely; while in case of need I had the means of making snowshoes and could retreat or hold my ground as I pleased.

Presently the storm broke forth into full snowy bloom, and the thronging crystals darkened the air. The wind swept past in hissing floods, grinding the snow into meal and sweeping down into the hollows in enormous drifts all the heavier particles, while the finer dust was sifted through the sky, increasing the icy gloom. But my fire glowed bravely as if in glad defiance of the drift to quench it, and, notwithstanding but little trace of my nest could be seen after the snow had leveled and buried it, I was snug and warm, and the passionate uproar produced a glad excitement.

Day after day the storm continued, piling snow on snow in weariless abundance. There were short periods of quiet, when the sun would seem to look eagerly down through rents in the clouds, as if to know how the work was advancing. During these calm intervals I replenished my fire — sometimes without leaving the nest, for fire and woodpile were so near this could easily be done — or busied myself with my notebook, watching the gestures of the trees in taking the snow, examining separate crystals under a lens, and learning the methods of their deposition as an enduring fountain for the streams. Several times, when the storm ceased for a few minutes, a Douglas squirrel came frisking from the foot of a clump of dwarf pines, moving in sudden interrupted spurts over the bossy snow; then, without any apparent guidance, he would dig rapidly into the drift where were buried some grains of barley that the horses had left. The Douglas squirrel does not strictly belong to these upper woods, and I was surprised to see him out in such weather. The mountain sheep also, quite a large flock of them, came to my camp and took shelter beside a clump of matted dwarf pines a little above my nest.

The storm lasted about a week, but before it was ended Sisson became alarmed and sent up the guide with animals to see what had become of me and recover the camp outfit. The news spread that "there was a man on the mountain," and he must surely have perished, and Sisson was blamed for allowing any one to attempt climbing in such weather; while I was as safe as anybody in the lowlands, lying like a squirrel in a warm, fluffy nest, busied about my own affairs and wishing only to be let alone. Later, however, a trail could not have been broken for a horse, and some of the camp furniture would have had to be abandoned. On the fifth day I returned to Sisson's, and from that comfortable base made excursions, as the weather permitted, to the Black Butte, to the foot of the Whitney Glacier, around the base of the mountain, to Rhett and Klamath Lakes, to the Modoc region and elsewhere, developing many interesting scenes and experiences.

But the next spring, on the other side of this eventful winter, I saw and felt still more of the Shasta snow. For then it was my fortune to get into the very heart of a storm, and to be held in it for a long time.

On the 28th of April [1875] I led a party up the mountain for the purpose of making a survey of the summit with reference to the location of the Geodetic monument. On the 30th, accompanied by Jerome Fay, I made another ascent to make some barometrical observations, the day intervening between the two ascents being devoted to establishing a camp on the extreme edge of the timber-line. Here, on our red trachyte bed, we obtained two hours of shallow sleep broken for occasional glimpses of the keen, starry night. At two o'clock we rose, breakfasted on a warmed tin-cupful of coffee and a piece of frozen venison broiled on the coals, and started for the summit. Up to this time there was nothing in sight that betokened the approach of a storm; but on gaining the summit, we saw toward Lassen's Butte hundreds of square miles of white cumuli boiling dreamily in the sunshine far beneath us, and causing no alarm.

The slight weariness of the ascent was soon rested away, and our glorious morning in the sky promised nothing but enjoyment. At 9 A.M. the dry thermometer stood at 34° in the shade and rose steadily until at 1 P.M. it stood at 50°, probably influenced somewhat by radiation from the sun-warmed cliffs. A common bumble-bee, not at all benumbed, zigzagged vigorously about our heads for a few moments, as if unconscious of the fact that the nearest honey flower was a mile beneath him

In the mean time clouds were growing down in Shasta Valley — massive swelling cumuli, displaying delicious tones of purple and gray in the hollows of their sun-beaten bosses. Extending gradually southward around on both sides of Shasta, these at length united with the older field towards Lassen's Butte, thus encircling Mount Shasta in one continu-

76

ous cloud-zone. Rhett and Kalmath Lakes
were eclipsed beneath clouds scarcely less brilliant than their own silvery disks. The Modoc
Lava Beds, many a snow-laden peak far north
in Oregon, the Scott and Trinity and Siskiyou
Mountains, the peaks of the Sierra, the blue
Coast Range, Shasta Valley, the dark forests
filling the valley of the Sacramento, all in turn
were obscured or buried, leaving the lofty cone
on which we stood solitary in the sunshine
between two skies — a sky of spotless blue
above, a sky of glittering cloud beneath. The
creative sun shone glorious on the vast expanse
of cloudland; hill and dale, mountain and valley springing into existence responsive to his
rays and steadily developing in beauty and
individuality. One huge mountain-cone of
cloud, corresponding to Mount Shasta in these
newborn cloud-ranges, rose close alongside
with a visible motion, its firm, polished bosses
seeming so near and substantial that we almost
fancied we might leap down upon them from
where we stood and make our way to the lowlands. No hint was given, by anything in
their appearance, of the fleeting character of
these most sublime and beautiful cloud mountains. On the contrary they impressed one as
being lasting additions to the landscape.

The weather of the springtime and summer,

throughout the Sierra in general, is usually varied by slight local rains and dustings of snow, most of which are obviously far too joyous and life-giving to be regarded as storms — single clouds growing in the sunny sky, ripening in an hour, showering the heated landscape, and passing away like a thought, leaving no visible bodily remains to stain the sky. Snowstorms of the same gentle kind abound among the high peaks, but in spring they not unfrequently attain larger proportions, assuming a violence and energy of expression scarcely surpassed by those bred in the depths of winter. Such was the storm now gathering about us.

It began to declare itself shortly after noon, suggesting to us the idea of at once seeking our safe camp in the timber and abandoning the purpose of making an observation of the barometer at 3 P.M., — two having already been made, at 9 A.M., and 12 M., while simultaneous observations were made at Strawberry Valley. Jerome peered at short intervals over the ridge, contemplating the rising clouds with anxious gestures in the rough wind, and at length declared that if we did not make a speedy escape we should be compelled to pass the rest of the day and night on the summit. But anxiety to complete my observations stifled my own instinctive promptings to re-

78

treat, and held me to my work. No inexperienced person was depending on me, and I told Jerome that we two mountaineers should be able to make our way down through any storm likely to fall.

Presently thin, fibrous films of cloud began to blow directly over the summit from north to south, drawn out in long fairy webs like carded wool, forming and dissolving as if by magic. The wind twisted them into ringlets and whirled them in a succession of graceful convolutions like the outside sprays of Yosemite Falls in flood-time; then, sailing out into the thin azure over the precipitous brink of the ridge they were drifted together like wreaths of foam on a river. These higher and finer cloud fabrics were evidently produced by the chilling of the air from its own expansion caused by the upward deflection of the wind against the slopes of the mountain. They steadily increased on the north rim of the cone, forming at length a thick, opaque, ill-defined embankment from the icy meshes of which snow-flowers began to fall, alternating with hail. The sky speedily darkened, and just as I had completed my last observation and boxed my instruments ready for the descent, the storm began in serious earnest. At first the cliffs were beaten with hail, every stone of which, as far as I could see, was regular in form, six-sided pyramids with rounded base, rich and sumptuous-looking, and fashioned with loving care, yet seemingly thrown away on those desolate crags down which they went rolling, falling, sliding in a network of curious streams.

After we had forced our way down the ridge and past the group of hissing fumaroles, the storm became inconceivably violent. The thermometer fell 22° in a few minutes, and soon dropped below zero. The hail gave place to snow, and darkness came on like night. The wind, rising to the highest pitch of violence, boomed and surged amid the desolate crags; lightning-flashes in quick succession cut the gloomy darkness; and the thunders, the most tremendously loud and appalling I ever heard, made an almost continuous roar, stroke following stroke in quick, passionate succession, as though the mountain were being rent to its foundations and the fires of the old volcano were breaking forth again.

Could we at once have begun to descend the snow-slopes leading to the timber, we might have made good our escape, however dark and wild the storm. As it was, we had first to make our way along a dangerous ridge nearly a mile and a half long, flanked in many places by steep ice-slopes at the head of the Whitney Glacier on one side and by shattered precipices on the other. Apprehensive of this coming darkness, I had taken the precaution, when the storm began, to make the most dangerous points clear to my mind, and to mark their relations with reference to the direction of the wind. When, therefore, the darkness came on, and the bewildering drift, I felt confident that we could force our way through it with no other guidance. After passing the "Hot Springs" I halted in the lee of a lava-block to let Jerome, who had fallen a little behind, come up. Here he opened a council in which, under circumstances sufficiently exciting but without evincing any bewilderment, he maintained, in opposition to my views, that it was impossible to proceed. He firmly refused to make the venture to find the camp, while I, aware of the dangers that would necessarily attend our efforts, and conscious of being the cause of his present peril, decided not to leave him.

Our discussions ended, Jerome made a dash from the shelter of the lava-block and began forcing his way back against the wind to the "Hot Springs," wavering and struggling to resist being carried away, as if he were fording a rapid stream. After waiting and watching in vain for some flaw in the storm that might be urged as a new argument in favor of attempting the descent, I was compelled to follow. "Here," said Jerome, as we shivered in the midst of the hissing, sputtering fumaroles, "we shall be safe from frost." "Yes," said I, "we can lie in this mud and steam and sludge, warm at least on one side; but how can we protect our lungs from the acid gases, and how, after our clothing is saturated, shall we be able to reach camp without freezing, even after the storm is over? We shall have to wait for sunshine, and when will it come?"

The tempered area to which we had committed ourselves extended over about one fourth of an acre; but it was only about an eighth of an inch in thickness, for the scalding gas-jets were shorn off close to the ground by the oversweeping flood of frosty wind. And how lavishly the snow fell only mountaineers may know. The crisp crystal flowers seemed to touch one another and fairly to thicken the tremendous blast that carried them. This was the bloom-time, the summer of the cloud, and never before have I seen even a mountain cloud flowering so profusely.

When the bloom of the Shasta chaparral is falling, the ground is sometimes covered for hundreds of square miles to a depth of half an inch. But the bloom of this fertile snow-cloud grew and matured and fell to a depth of two

feet in a few hours. Some crystals landed with
their rays almost perfect, but most of them
were worn and broken by striking against one
another, or by rolling on the ground. The
touch of these snow-flowers in calm weather is
infinitely gentle — glinting, swaying, settling
silently in the dry mountain air, or massed in
flakes soft and downy. To lie out alone in the
mountains of a still night and be touched by
the first of these small silent messengers from
the sky is a memorable experience, and the
fineness of that touch none will forget. But
the storm-blast laden with crisp, sharp snow
seems to crush and bruise and stupefy with its
multitude of stings, and compels the bravest
to turn and flee.

The snow fell without abatement until an
hour or two after what seemed to be the natural darkness of the night. Up to the time the
storm first broke on the summit its development was remarkably gentle. There was a
deliberate growth of clouds, a weaving of
translucent tissue above, then the roar of the
wind and the thunder, and the darkening flight
of snow. Its subsidence was not less sudden.
The clouds broke and vanished, not a crystal
was left in the sky, and the stars shone out with
pure and tranquil radiance.

During the storm we lay on our backs so as

to present as little surface as possible to the wind, and to let the drift pass over us. The mealy snow sifted into the folds of our clothing and in many places reached the skin. We were glad at first to see the snow packing about us, hoping it would deaden the force of the wind, but it soon froze into a stiff, crusty heap as the temperature fell, rather augmenting our novel misery.

When the heat became unendurable, on some spot where steam was escaping through the sludge, we tried to stop it with snow and mud, or shifted a little at a time by shoving with our heels; for to stand in blank exposure to the fearful wind in our frozen-and-broiled condition seemed certain death. The acrid incrustations sublimed from the escaping gases frequently gave way, opening new vents to scald us; and, fearing that if at any time the wind should fall, carbonic acid, which often formed a considerable portion of the gaseous exhalations of volcanoes, might collect in sufficient quantities to cause sleep and death, I warned Jerome against forgetting himself for a single moment, even should his sufferings admit of such a thing.

Accordingly, when during the long, dreary watches of the night we roused from a state of half-consciousness, we called each other by name in a frightened, startled way, each fearing the other might be benumbed or dead. The ordinary sensations of cold give but a faint conception of that which comes on after hard climbing with want of food and sleep in such exposure as this. Life is then seen to be a fire, that now smoulders, now brightens, and may be easily quenched. The weary hours wore away like dim half-forgotten years, so long and eventful they seemed, though we did nothing but suffer. Still the pain was not always of that bitter, intense kind that precludes thought and takes away all capacity for enjoyment. A sort of dreamy stupor came on at times in which we fancied we saw dry, resinous logs suitable for campfires, just as after going days without food men fancy they see bread.

Frozen, blistered, famished, benumbed, our bodies seemed lost to us at times — all dead but the eyes. For the duller and fainter we became the clearer was our vision, though only in momentary glimpses. Then, after the sky cleared, we gazed at the stars, blessed immortals of light, shining with marvelous brightness with long lance rays, near-looking and new-looking, as if never seen before. Again they would look familiar and remind us of stargazing at home. Oftentimes imagination coming into play would present charming pictures of the warm zone below, mingled with others near and far. Then the bitter wind and the drift would break the blissful vision and dreary pains cover us like clouds. "Are you suffering much?" Jerome would inquire with pitiful faintness. "Yes," I would say, striving to keep my voice brave, "frozen and burned; but never mind, Jerome, the night will wear away at last, and to-morrow we go a-Maying, and what campfires we will make, and what sun-baths we will take!"

The frost grew more and more intense, and we became icy and covered over with a crust of frozen snow, as if we had lain cast away in the drift all winter. In about thirteen hours — every hour like a year — day began to dawn, but it was long ere the summit's rocks were touched by the sun. No clouds were visible from where we lay, yet the morning was dull and blue, and bitterly frosty; and hour after hour passed by while we eagerly watched the pale light stealing down the ridge to the hollow where we lay. But there was not a trace of that warm, flushing sunrise splendor we so long had hoped for.

As the time drew near to make an effort to reach camp, we became concerned to know what strength was left us, and whether or no we could walk; for we had lain flat all this time without once rising to our feet. Mountaineers, however, always find in themselves a reserve of power after great exhaustion. It is a kind of second life, available only in emergencies like this; and, having proved its existence, I had no great fear that either of us would fail, though one of my arms was already benumbed and hung powerless.

At length, after the temperature was somewhat mitigated on this memorable first of May, we arose and began to struggle homeward. Our frozen trousers could scarcely be made to bend at the knee, and we waded the snow with difficulty. The summit ridge was fortunately wind-swept and nearly bare, so we were not compelled to lift our feet high, and on reaching the long home slopes laden with loose snow we made rapid progress, sliding and shuffling and pitching headlong, our feebleness accelerating rather than diminishing our speed. When we had descended some three thousand feet the sunshine warmed our backs and we began to revive. At 10 A.M. we reached the timber and were safe.

Half an hour later we heard Sisson shouting down among the firs, coming with horses to take us to the hotel. After breaking a trail through the snow as far as possible he had tied his animals and walked up. We had been so long without food that we cared but little about eating, but we eagerly drank the coffee he prepared for us. Our feet were frozen, and thawing them was painful, and had to be done very slowly by keeping them buried in soft snow for several hours, which avoided permanent damage. Five thousand feet below the summit we found only three inches of new snow, and at the base of the mountain only a slight shower of rain had fallen, showing how local our storm had been, notwithstanding its terrific fury. Our feet were wrapped in sacking, and we were soon mounted and on our way down into the thick sunshine — "God's Country," as Sisson calls the Chaparral Zone. In two hours' ride the last snow-bank was left behind. Violets appeared along the edges of the trail, and the chaparral was coming into bloom, with young lilies and larkspurs about the open places in rich profusion. How beautiful seemed the golden sunbeams streaming through the woods between the warm brown boles of the cedars and pines! All my friends among the birds and plants seemed like *old* friends, and we felt like speaking to every one of them as we passed, as if we had been a long time away in some far, strange country.

In the afternoon we reached Strawberry Valley and fell asleep. Next morning we seemed to have risen from the dead. My bedroom was flooded with sunshine, and from the window I saw the great white Shasta cone clad in forests and clouds and bearing them loftily in the sky. Everything seemed full and radiant with the freshness and beauty and enthusiasm of youth. Sisson's children came in with flowers and covered my bed, and the storm on the mountaintop vanished like a dream.

WITH the exception of a few spires and pinnacles, the South Dome is the only rock about the Valley that is strictly inaccessible without artificial means, and its inaccessibility is expressed in severe terms. Nevertheless many a mountaineer, gazing admiringly, tried hard to invent a way to the top of its noble crown — all in vain, until in the year 1875, George Anderson, an indomitable Scotchman, undertook the adventure.

The side facing Tenaya Cañon is an absolutely vertical precipice from the summit to a depth of about sixteen hundred feet, and on the opposite side it is nearly vertical for about as great a depth. The southwest side presents a very steep and finely drawn curve from the top down a thousand feet or more, while on the northeast, where it is united with the Clouds' Rest Ridge, one may easily reach a point called the Saddle, about seven hundred feet below the summit. From the Saddle the Dome rises in a graceful curve a few degrees too steep for unaided climbing,

91

besides being defended by overleaning ends of the concentric dome layers of the granite.

A year or two before Anderson gained the summit, John Conway, the master trail-builder of the Valley, and his little sons, who climbed smooth rocks like lizards, made a bold effort to reach the top by climbing barefooted up the grand curve with a rope which they fastened at irregular intervals by means of eye-bolts driven into joints of the rock. But finding that the upper part would require laborious drilling, they abandoned the attempt, glad to escape from the dangerous position they had reached, some three hundred feet above the Saddle. Anderson began with Conway's old rope, which had been left in place, and resolutely drilled his way to the top, inserting eye-bolts five to six feet apart, and making his rope fast to each in succession, resting his feet on the last bolt while he drilled a hole for the next above. Occasionally some irregularity in the curve, or slight foothold, would enable him to climb a few feet without a rope, which he would pass and begin drilling again, and thus the whole work was accomplished in a few days. From this slender beginning he proposed to construct a substantial stairway which he hoped to complete in time for the next year's travel, but while busy getting out timber for his stairway

92

and dreaming of the wealth he hoped to gain
from tolls, he was taken sick and died all alone
in his little cabin.

On the 10th of November, after returning
from a visit to Mount Shasta, a month or two
after Anderson had gained the summit, I made
haste to the Dome, not only for the pleasure of
climbing, but to see what I might learn. The
first winter storm clouds had blossomed and
the mountains and all the high points about
the Valley were mantled in fresh snow. I was,
therefore, a little apprehensive of danger from
the slipperiness of the rope and the rock. Anderson himself tried to prevent me from making
the attempt, refusing to believe that any one
could climb his rope in the snow-muffled condition in which it then was. Moreover, the sky
was overcast and solemn snow clouds began
to curl around the summit, and my late experiences on icy Shasta came to mind. But reflecting that I had matches in my pocket, and that
I might find a little firewood, I concluded that
in case of a storm the night could be spent on
the Dome without any suffering worth minding,
no matter what the clouds might bring forth.
I therefore pushed on and gained the top.

It was one of those brooding, changeful days
that come between the Indian summer and
winter, when the leaf colors have grown dim

and the clouds come and go among the cliffs like
living creatures looking for work: now hovering
aloft, now caressing rugged rock brows with
great gentleness, or, wandering afar over the
tops of the forests, touching the spires of fir and
pine with their soft silken fringes as if trying to
tell the glad news of the coming of snow.

The first view was perfectly glorious. A massive cloud of pure pearl luster, apparently as
fixed and calm as the meadows and groves in
the shadow beneath it, was arched across the
Valley from wall to wall, one end resting on the
grand abutment of El Capitan, the other on
Cathedral Rock. A little later, as I stood on
the tremendous verge overlooking Mirror Lake,
a flock of smaller clouds, white as snow, came
from the north, trailing their downy skirts over
the dark forests, and entered the Valley with
solemn god-like gestures through Indian Cañon
and over the North Dome and Royal Arches,
moving swiftly, yet with majestic deliberation.
On they came, nearer and nearer, gathering and
massing beneath my feet and filling the Tenaya Cañon. Then the sun shone free, lighting
the pearly gray surface of the cloud-like sea
and making it glow. Gazing, admiring, I was
startled to see for the first time the rare optical
phenomenon of the "Specter of the Brocken."
My shadow, clearly outlined, about half a

mile long, lay upon this glorious white surface
with startling effect. I walked back and forth,
waved my arms and struck all sorts of atti-
tudes, to see every slightest movement enor-
mously exaggerated. Considering that I have
looked down so many times from mountain-
tops on seas of all sorts of clouds, it seems
strange that I should have seen the "Brocken
Specter" only this once. A grander surface and
a grander standpoint, however, could hardly
have been found in all the Sierra.

After this grand show the cloud sea rose
higher, wreathing the Dome and submerging it
for a short time, making darkness like night,
and I began to think of looking for a camp-
ground in a cluster of dwarf pines. But soon
the sun shone free again, the clouds, sinking
lower and lower, gradually vanished, leaving
the Valley with its Indian-summer colors apparently refreshed, while to the eastward the
summit peaks, clad in new snow, towered along
the horizon in glorious array.

Though apparently it is perfectly bald, there
are four clumps of pines growing on the summit, representing three species, *Pinus albicaulis, P. contorta* and *P. ponderosa,* var. *Jeffreyi* —
all three, of course, repressed and storm-beaten.
The alpine spiræa grows here also and blossoms
profusely with potentilla, erigeron, eriogonum,

pentstemon, solidago, an interesting species of onion, and four or five of grasses and sedges. None of these differs in any respect from those of other summits of the same height, excepting the curious little narrow-leaved, waxen-bulbed onion, which I had not seen elsewhere.

Notwithstanding the enthusiastic eagerness of tourists to reach the crown of the Dome, the views of the Valley from this lofty standpoint are less striking than from many other points comparatively low, chiefly on account of the foreshortening effect produced by looking down from so great a height. The North Dome is dwarfed almost beyond recognition, the grand sculpture of the Royal Arches is scarcely noticeable, and the whole range of walls on both sides seem comparatively low, especially when the Valley is flooded with noon sunshine; while the Dome itself, the most sublime feature of all the Yosemite views, is out of sight beneath one's feet. The view of Little Yosemite Valley is very fine, though inferior to one obtained from the base of the Starr King Cone, but the summit landscapes toward Mounts Ritter, Lyell, Dana, Conness, and the Merced group, are very effective and complete.

No one has attempted to carry out Anderson's plan of making the Dome accessible. For my part I should prefer leaving it in pure wildness, though, after all, no great damage could be done by tramping over it. The surface would be strewn with tin cans and bottles, but the winter gales would blow the rubbish away. Avalanches might strip off any sort of stairway or ladder that might be built. Blue jays and Clark crows have trodden the Dome for many a day, and so have beetles and chipmunks, and Tissiack would hardly be more "conquered" or spoiled should man be added to her list of visitors. His louder scream and heavier scrambling would not stir a line of her countenance.

When the sublime ice floods of the glacial period poured down the flank of the range over what is now Yosemite Valley, they were compelled to break through a dam of domes extending across from Mount Starr King to North Dome; and as the period began to draw near a close the shallowing ice currents were divided and the South Dome was, perhaps, the first to emerge, burnished and shining like a mirror above the surface of the icy sea; and though it has sustained the wear and tear of the elements tens of thousands of years, it yet remains a telling monument of the action of the great glaciers that brought it to light. Its entire surface is still covered with glacial hieroglyphics whose interpretation is the reward of all who devoutly study them.

MOUNTAIN THOUGHTS

1872 (?).

The Sierra. Mountains holy as Sinai. No mountains I know of are so alluring. None so hospitable, kindly, tenderly inspiring. It seems strange that everybody does not come at their call. They are given, like the Gospel, without money and without price. ' 'Tis heaven alone that is given away.'

Here is calm so deep, grasses cease waving. . . . Wonderful how completely everything in wild nature fits into us, as if truly part and parent of us. The sun shines not on us but in us. The rivers flow not past, but through us, thrilling, tingling, vibrating every fiber and cell of the substance of our bodies, making them glide and sing. The trees wave and the flowers bloom in our bodies as well as our souls, and every bird song, wind song, and tremendous storm song of the rocks in the heart of the mountains is our song, our very own, and sings our love.

The Song of God, sounding on forever. So pure and sure and universal is the harmony, it matters not where we are, where we strike in on the wild lowland plains. We care not to go to the mountains, and on the mountains we care not to go to the plains. But as soon as we are absorbed in the

99

harmony, plain, mountain, calm, storm, lilies and sequoias, forests and meads are only different strands of many-colored Light—are one in the sunbeam!

What wonders lie in every mountain day! . . . Crystals of snow, plash of small raindrops, hum of small insects, booming beetles, the jolly rattle of grasshoppers, chirping crickets, the screaming of hawks, jays, and Clark crows, the 'coo-r-r-r' of cranes, the honking of geese, partridges drumming, trumpeting swans, frogs croaking, the whirring rattle of snakes, the awful enthusiasm of booming falls, the roar of cataracts, the crash and roll of thunder, earthquake shocks, the whisper of rills soothing to slumber, the piping of marmots, the bark of squirrels, the laugh of a wolf, the snorting of deer, the explosive roaring of bears, the squeak of mice, the cry of the loon— loneliest, wildest of sounds. . . .

A fine place for feasting if only one be poor enough. One is speedily absorbed into the spiritual values of things. The body vanishes and the freed soul goes abroad. . . .

Only in the roar of storms do these mighty solitudes find voice at all commensurate with their grandeur. . . . The pines at the approach of storms show eager expectancy, bowing, swishing, tossing their branches with eager gestures, roaring like lions about to be fed, standing bent and round-shouldered like sentinels exposed. . . .

Sickness, pain, death — yet who could guess their existence in this fresh, abounding, overflowing life, this universal beauty?

Race living on race, killers killed, yet how little we see of this slaughter! How neatly, secretly, decently is this killing done! I never saw one drop of blood, one red stain on all this wilderness. Even death is in harmony here. Only in shambles and the downy beds of homes is death terrible. Perhaps there is more pleasure than pain in natural death, or even violent death. Livingstone declared that the crushing of his arm by a lion was rather pleasurable than otherwise. . . .

Bloody Canyon. Nature's darlings are cared for and caressed even here, and protected by a thousand miracles in the very home and brooding-places of storms.

Faint are the marks of any kind of life, and at first you cannot see them or feel them at all. But here is the blessed water-ouzel pleading, fluttering about amid the spray, and blending his sweet, small, human songs with those of the streams he loves so well. And many other birds who build their nests here, and the flowers with few leaves that bloom on the rocks as if fallen like snow from the sky.

And here the grasshopper jumps and springs his rattle, as if to say, 'Who is afraid?'

And the bumblebee singing every summer the songs sung a thousand years ago.

A flock of wild sheep move aloft on the crags of the walls, not lost and cast away, but seeming to say in fullness of strength and ease: 'Here we are fled, and here is our home and safe hiding-place.'

One thinks of the redmen with flesh colored like the rocks, and sinews tough as the granite, who for thousands of years have dragged in files through these silent depths, clad in dull skins and grass, with mountain flowers stuck in their black hair and their wild animal eyes sparkling bright as the lakes.

Only the unimaginative can fail to feel the enchantment of these mountains.

Nothing is more wonderful than to find smooth harmony in this lofty cragged region where at first sight all seems so rough. From any of the high standpoints a thousand peaks, pinnacles, spires are seen thrust into the sky and so sheer and bare as to be inaccessible to wild sheep, accessible only to the eagle. Any one by itself harsh, rugged, crumbling, yet in connection with others seems like a line of writing along the sky; it melts into melody, one leading into another, keeping rhythm in time.

The cleanness of the ground suggests Nature

taking pains like a housewife, the rock pavements seem as if carefully swept and dusted and polished every day. No wonder one feels a magic exhilaration when these pavements are touched, when the manifold currents of life that flow through the pores of the rock are considered, that keep every crystal particle in rhythmic motion dancing.

Tissiacks seldom have lofty domes to give grace to their strength. They are mostly stout, thickset mountains with spread bases for strength, because they have been born of two great streams and overflowed and much eroded. Glaciers eat their own offspring.

Books. I have a low opinion of books; they are but piles of stones set up to show coming travelers where other minds have been, or at best signal smokes to call attention. Cadmus and all the other inventors of letters receive a thousand-fold more credit than they deserve. No amount of word-making will ever make a single soul to *know* these mountains. As well seek to warm the naked and frostbitten by lectures on caloric and pictures of flame. One day's exposure to mountains is better than cartloads of books. See how willingly Nature poses herself upon photographers' plates. No earthly chemicals are so sensitive as those of the human soul. All that is required is exposure, and purity of material. 'The pure in heart shall see God!'...

Water Music. When in making our way through a forest we hear the loud boom of a waterfall, we know that the stream is descending a precipice. If a heavy rumble and roar, then we know it is passing over a craggy incline. But not only are the existence and size of these larger characters of its channel proclaimed, but all the others. Go to the fountain-canyons of the Merced. Some portions of its channel will appear smooth, others rough, here a slope, there a vertical wall, here a sandy meadow, there a lake-bowl, and the young river speaks and sings all the smaller characters of the smooth slope and downy hush of meadow as faithfully as it sings the great precipices and rapid inclines, so that anyone who has learned the language of running water will see its character in the dark.

Beside the grand history of the glaciers and their own, the mountain streams sing the history of every avalanche or earthquake and of snow, all easily recognized by the human ear, and every word evoked by the falling leaf and drinking deer, beside a thousand other facts so small and spoken by the stream in so low a voice the human ear cannot hear them. Thus every event is written and spoken. The wing scars the sky, making a

MOUNTAIN THOUGHTS

path inevitably as the deer in snow, and the
winds all know it and tell it though we hear it not.

AMBITIOUS climbers, seeking adventures and opportunities to test their strength and skill, occasionally attempt to penetrate the wilderness on the west side of the Sound, and push on to the summit of Mount Olympus. But the grandest excursion of all to be made hereabouts is to Mount Rainier, to climb to the top of its icy crown. The mountain is very high,[1] fourteen thousand four hundred feet, and laden with glaciers that are terribly roughened and interrupted by crevasses and ice-cliffs. Only good climbers should attempt to gain the summit, led by a guide of proved nerve and endurance. A good trail has been cut through the woods to the base of the mountain on the north; but the summit of the mountain never has been reached from this side, though many brave attempts have been made upon it.

MOUNTAINEERING ESSAYS

Last summer I gained the summit from the south side, in a day and a half from the timber-line, without encountering any desperate obstacles that could not in some way be passed in good weather. I was accompanied by Keith, the artist, Professor Ingraham, and five ambitious young climbers from Seattle. We were led by the veteran mountaineer and guide Van Trump, of Yelm, who many years before guided General Stevens in his memorable ascent, and later Mr. Bailey, of Oakland. With a cumbersome abundance of campstools and blankets we set out from Seattle, traveling by rail as far as Yelm Prairie, on the Tacoma and Oregon road. Here we made our first camp and arranged with Mr. Longmire, a farmer in the neighborhood, for pack and saddle animals. The noble King Mountain was in full view from here, glorifying the bright, sunny day with his presence, rising in godlike majesty over the woods, with the magnificent prairie as a foreground. The distance to the mountain from Yelm in a straight line is perhaps fifty miles; but by the mule and yellow-jacket trail we had to follow it is a hundred miles. For, notwithstanding a portion of this trail runs in the air, where the wasps work hardest, it is far from being an air-line as commonly understood.

AN ASCENT OF MOUNT RAINIER

By night of the third day we reached the
Soda Springs on the right bank of the Nisqually, which goes roaring by, gray with mud,
gravel, and boulders from the caves of the
glaciers of Rainier, now close at hand. The
distance from the Soda Springs to the Camp
of the Clouds is about ten miles. The first
part of the way lies up the Nisqually Cañon,
the bottom of which is flat in some places and
the walls very high and precipitous, like those
of the Yosemite Valley. The upper part of
the cañon is still occupied by one of the Nisqually glaciers, from which this branch of the
river draws its source, issuing from a cave in
the gray, rock-strewn snout. About a mile
below the glacier we had to ford the river,
which caused some anxiety, for the current
is very rapid and carried forward large boulders as well as lighter material, while its savage
roar is bewildering.

At this point we left the cañon, climbing
out of it by a steep zigzag up the old lateral
moraine of the glacier, which was deposited
when the present glacier flowed past at this
height, and is about eight hundred feet high.
It is now covered with a superb growth of
Picea amabilis; [1] so also is the corresponding

[1] Doubtless the red silver fir, now classified as *Abies amabilis.* [Editor.]

109

portion of the right lateral. From the top of
the moraine, still ascending, we passed for a
mile or two through a forest of mixed growth,
mainly silver fir, Patton spruce, and mountain
pine, and then came to the charming park
region, at an elevation of about five thousand
feet above sea-level. Here the vast continuous woods at length begin to give way under
the dominion of climate, though still at this
height retaining their beauty and giving no
sign of stress of storm, sweeping upward in
belts of varying width, composed mainly of one
species of fir, sharp and spiry in form, leaving smooth, spacious parks, with here and
there separate groups of trees standing out in
the midst of the openings like islands in a lake.
Every one of these parks, great and small, is
a garden filled knee-deep with fresh, lovely
flowers of every hue, the most luxuriant and
the most extravagantly beautiful of all the
alpine gardens I ever beheld in all my mountain-top wanderings.

We arrived at the Cloud Camp at noon, but
no clouds were in sight, save a few gauzy
ornamental wreaths adrift in the sunshine.
Out of the forest at last there stood the mountain, wholly unveiled, awful in bulk and majesty, filling all the view like a separate, newborn world, yet withal so fine and so beautiful

it might well fire the dullest observer to desperate enthusiasm. Long we gazed in silent admiration, buried in tall daisies and anemones by the side of a snowbank. Higher we could not go with the animals and find food for them and wood for our own camp-fires, for just beyond this lies the region of ice, with only here and there an open spot on the ridges in the midst of the ice, with dwarf alpine plants, such as saxifrages and drabas, which reach far up between the glaciers, and low mats of the beautiful bryanthus, while back of us were the gardens and abundance of everything that heart could wish. Here we lay all the afternoon, considering the lilies and the lines of the mountains with reference to a way to the summit.

At noon next day we left camp and began our long climb. We were in light marching order, save one who pluckily determined to carry his camera to the summit. At night, after a long easy climb over wide and smooth fields of ice, we reached a narrow ridge, at an elevation of about ten thousand feet above the sea, on the divide between the glaciers of the Nisqually and the Cowlitz. Here we lay as best we could, waiting for another day, without fire of course, as we were now many miles beyond the timber-line and without much to cover us. After eating a little hardtack, each of us leveled a spot to lie on among lava-blocks and cinders. The night was cold, and the wind coming down upon us in stormy surges drove gritty ashes and fragments of pumice about our ears while chilling to the bone. Very short and shallow was our sleep that night; but day dawned at last, early rising was easy, and there was nothing about breakfast to cause any delay. About four o'clock we were off, and climbing began in earnest. We followed up the ridge on which we had spent the night, now along its crest, now on either side, or on the ice leaning against it, until we came to where it becomes massive and precipitous. Then we were compelled to crawl along a seam or narrow shelf, on its face, which we traced to its termination in the base of the great ice-cap. From this point all the climbing was over ice, which was here desperately steep but fortunately was at the same time carved into innumerable spikes and pillars which afforded good footholds, and we crawled cautiously on, warm with ambition and exercise.

At length, after gaining the upper extreme of our guiding ridge, we found a good place to rest and prepare ourselves to scale the dangerous upper curves of the dome. The surface almost everywhere was bare, hard, snowless ice, extremely slippery; and, though smooth in general, it was interrupted by a network of yawning crevasses, outspread like lines of defense against any attempt to win the summit. Here every one of the party took off his shoes and drove stout steel caulks about half an inch long into them, having brought tools along for the purpose, and not having made use of them until now so that the points might not get dulled on the rocks ere the smooth, dangerous ice was reached. Besides being well shod each carried an alpenstock, and for special difficulties we had a hundred feet of rope and an axe.

Thus prepared, we stepped forth afresh, slowly groping our way through tangled lines of crevasses, crossing on snow bridges here and there after cautiously testing them, jumping at narrow places, or crawling around the ends of the largest, bracing well at every point with our alpenstocks and setting our spiked shoes squarely down on the dangerous slopes. It was nerve-trying work, most of it, but we made good speed nevertheless, and by noon all stood together on the utmost summit, save one who, his strength failing for a time, came up later.

We remained on the summit nearly two hours, looking about us at the vast maplike views, comprehending hundreds of miles of the Cascade Range, with their black interminable forests and white volcanic cones in glorious array reaching far into Oregon; the Sound region also, and the great plains of eastern Washington, hazy and vague in the distance. Clouds began to gather. Soon of all the land only the summits of the mountains, St. Helen's, Adams, and Hood, were left in sight, forming islands in the sky. We found two well-formed and well-preserved craters on the summit, lying close together like two plates on a table with their rims touching. The highest point of the mountain is located between the craters, where their edges come in contact. Sulphurous fumes and steam issue from several vents, giving out a sickening smell that can be detected at a considerable distance. The unwasted condition of these craters, and, indeed, to a great extent, of the entire mountain, would tend to show that Rainier is still a comparatively young mountain. With the exception of the projecting lips of the craters and the top of a subordinate summit a short distance to the northward, the mountain is solidly capped with ice all around; and it is this ice-cap which forms the grand central fountain whence all the twenty glaciers of Rainier flow, radiating in every direction.

AN ASCENT OF MOUNT RAINIER

The descent was accomplished without disaster, though several of the party had narrow escapes. One slipped and fell, and as he shot past me seemed to be going to certain death. So steep was the ice-slope no one could move to help him, but fortunately, keeping his presence of mind, he threw himself on his face and digging his alpenstock into the ice, gradually retarded his motion until he came to rest. Another broke through a slim bridge over a crevasse, but his momentum at the time carried him against the lower edge and only his alpenstock was lost in the abyss. Thus crippled by the loss of his staff, we had to lower him the rest of the way down the dome by means of the rope we carried. Falling rocks from the upper precipitous part of the ridge were also a source of danger, as they came whizzing past in successive volleys; but none told on us, and when we at length gained the gentle slopes of the lower ice-fields, we ran and slid at our ease, making fast, glad time, all care and danger past, and arrived at our beloved Cloud Camp before sundown.

We were rather weak from want of nourishment, and some suffered from sunburn, notwithstanding the partial protection of glasses and veils; otherwise, all were unscathed and well. The view we enjoyed from the summit could hardly be surpassed in sublimity and grandeur; but one feels far from home so high in the sky, so much so that one is inclined to guess that, apart from the acquisition of knowledge and the exhilaration of climbing, more pleasure is to be found at the foot of mountains than on their frozen tops. Doubly happy, however, is the man to whom lofty mountain-tops are within reach, for the lights that shine there illumine all that lies below.

THE most interesting of the short excursions we made from Fort Wrangell was the one up the Stickeen River to the head of steam navigation. From Mt. St. Elias the Coast Range extends in a broad, lofty chain beyond the southern boundary of the territory, gashed by stupendous cañons, each of which carries a lively river, though most of them are comparatively short, as their highest sources lie in the icy solitudes of the range within forty or fifty miles of the coast. A few, however, of these foaming, roaring streams — the Alsek, Chilcat, Chilcoot, Taku, Stickeen, and perhaps others — head beyond the range with some of the southwest branches of the Mackenzie and Yukon.

The largest side branches of the main-trunk cañons of all these mountain streams are still occupied by glaciers which descend in showy ranks, their massy, bulging snouts lying back a little distance in the shadows of the walls, or pushing forward among the cotton-woods that line the banks of the rivers, or even stretching all the way across the main cañons, compelling the rivers to find a channel beneath them.

The Stickeen was, perhaps, the best known of the rivers that cross the Coast Range, because it was the best way to the Mackenzie River Cassiar gold-mines. It is about three hundred and fifty miles long, and is navigable for small steamers a hundred and fifty miles to Glenora, and sometimes to Telegraph Creek, fifteen miles farther. It first pursues a westerly course through grassy plains darkened here and there with groves of spruce and pine; then, curving southward and receiving numerous tributaries from the north, it enters the Coast Range, and sweeps across it through a magnificent cañon three thousand to five thousand feet deep, and more than a hundred miles long. The majestic cliffs and mountains forming the cañon walls display endless variety of form and sculpture, and are wonderfully adorned and enlivened with glaciers and waterfalls, while throughout almost its whole extent the floor is a flowery landscape garden, like Yosemite. The most striking features are the glaciers, hanging over the cliffs, descending the side cañons and pushing forward to the river, greatly enhancing the wild beauty of all the others.

Gliding along the swift-flowing river, the views change with bewildering rapidity. Wonderful, too, are the changes dependent on the seasons and the weather. In spring, when the snow is melting fast, you enjoy the countless rejoicing waterfalls; the gentle breathing of warm winds; the colors of the young leaves and flowers when the bees are busy and wafts of fragrance are drifting hither and thither from miles of wild roses, clover, and honeysuckle; the swaths of birch and willow on the lower slopes following the melting of the winter avalanche snow-banks; the bossy cumuli swelling in white and purple piles above the highest peaks; gray rain-clouds wreathing the outstanding brows and battlements of the walls; and the breaking-forth of the sun after the rain; the shining of the leaves and streams and crystal architecture of the glaciers; the rising of fresh fragrance; the song of the happy birds; and the serene color-grandeur of the morning and evening sky. In summer you find the groves and gardens in full dress; glaciers melting rapidly under sunshine and rain; waterfalls in all their glory; the river rejoicing in its strength; young birds trying their wings; bears enjoying salmon and berries; all the life of the cañon brimming full like the streams. In autumn comes rest, as if the year's work were done. The rich, hazy sunshine streaming over the cliffs calls forth the last of the gentians and goldenrods; the groves and thickets and meadows bloom again as their leaves change to red and yellow petals; the rocks also, and the glaciers, seem to bloom like the plants in the mellow golden light. And so goes the song, change succeeding change in sublime harmony through all the wonderful seasons and weather.

My first trip up the river was made in the spring with the missionary party soon after our arrival at Wrangell. We left Wrangell in the afternoon and anchored for the night above the river delta, and started up the river early next morning when the heights above the "Big Stickeen" Glacier and the smooth domes and copings and arches of solid snow along the tops of the cañon walls were glowing in the early beams. We arrived before noon at the old trading-post called "Buck's" in front of the Stickeen Glacier, and remained long enough to allow the few passengers who wished a nearer view to cross the river to the terminal moraine. The sunbeams streaming through the ice pinnacles along its terminal wall produced a wonderful glory of color, and the broad, sparkling crystal prairie and the distant snowy fountains were wonderfully- attractive and made me pray for opportunity to explore them.

Of the many glaciers, a hundred or more, that adorn the walls of the great Stickeen River Cañon, this is the largest. It draws its sources from snowy mountains within fifteen or twenty miles of the coast, pours through a comparatively narrow cañon about two miles in width in a magnificent cascade, and expands in a broad fan five or six miles in width, separated from the Stickeen River by its broad terminal moraine, fringed with spruces and willows. Around the beautifully drawn curve of the moraine the Stickeen River flows, having evidently been shoved by the glacier out of its direct course. On the opposite side of the cañon another somewhat smaller glacier, which now terminates four or five miles from the river, was once united front to front with the greater glacier, though at first both were tributaries of the main Stickeen Glacier which once filled the whole grand cañon. After the main trunk cañon was melted out, its side branches, drawing their sources from a height of three or four to five or six thousand feet, were cut off, and of course became separate glaciers,

121

occupying cirques and branch cañons along the tops and sides of the walls. The Indians have a tradition that the river used to run through a tunnel under the united fronts of the two large tributary glaciers mentioned above, which entered the main cañon from either side; and that on one occasion an Indian, anxious to get rid of his wife, had her sent adrift in a canoe down through the ice tunnel, expecting that she would trouble him no more. But to his surprise she floated through under the ice in safety. All the evidence connected with the present appearance of these two glaciers indicates that they were united and formed a dam across the river after the smaller tributaries had been melted off and had receded to a greater or lesser height above the valley floor.

The Big Stickeen Glacier is hardly out of sight ere you come upon another that pours a majestic crystal flood through the evergreens, while almost every hollow and tributary cañon contains a smaller one, the size, of course, varying with the extent of the area drained. Some are like mere snow-banks; others, with the blue ice apparent, depend in massive bulging curves and swells, and graduate into the river-like forms that maze through the lower forested regions and are so striking and beautiful that they are admired even by the passing miners with gold-dust in their eyes.

Thirty-five miles above the Big Stickeen Glacier is the "Dirt Glacier," the second in size. Its outlet is a fine stream, abounding in trout. On the opposite side of the river there is a group of five glaciers, one of them descending to within a hundred feet of the river.

Near Glenora, on the northeastern flank of the main Coast Range, just below a narrow gorge called "The Cañon," terraces first make their appearance, where great quantities of moraine material have been swept through the flood-choked gorge and of course outspread and deposited on the first open levels below. Here, too, occurs a marked change in climate and consequently in forests and general appearance of the face of the country. On account of destructive fires the woods are younger and are composed of smaller trees about a foot to eighteen inches in diameter and seventy-five feet high, mostly two-leaved pines which hold their seeds for several years after they are ripe. The woods here are without a trace of those deep accumulations of mosses, leaves, and decaying trunks which make so damp and unclearable a mass in the coast forests. Whole mountain-sides are covered with gray moss and lichens where the forest has been utterly destroyed. The river-bank cotton-woods are also smaller, and the birch and contorta pines mingle freely with the coast hemlock and spruce. The birch is common on the lower slopes and is very effective, its round, leafy, pale-green head contrasting with the dark, narrow spires of the conifers and giving a striking character to the forest. The "tamarac pine" or black pine, as the variety of *P. contorta* is called here, is yellowish-green, in marked contrast with the dark, lichen-draped spruce which grows above the pine at a height of about two thousand feet, in groves and belts where it has escaped fire and snow avalanches. There is another handsome spruce hereabouts, *Picea alba*, very slender and graceful in habit, drooping at the top like a mountain hemlock. I saw fine specimens a hundred and twenty-five feet high on deep bottom land a few miles below Glenora. The tops of some of them were almost covered with dense clusters of yellow and brown cones.

We reached the old Hudson's Bay trading-post at Glenora about one o'clock, and the captain informed me that he would stop here until the next morning, when he would make an early start for Wrangell.

At a distance of about seven or eight miles to the northeastward of the landing, there is an outstanding group of mountains crowning a spur from the main chain of the Coast Range, whose highest point rises about eight thousand feet above the level of the sea; and as Glenora is only a thousand feet above the sea, the height to be overcome in climbing this peak is about seven thousand feet. Though the time was short I determined to climb it, because of the advantageous position it occupied for general views of the peaks and glaciers of the east side of the great range.

Although it was now twenty minutes past three and the days were getting short, I thought that by rapid climbing I could reach the summit before sunset, in time to get a general view and a few pencil sketches, and make my way back to the steamer in the night. Mr. Young, one of the missionaries, asked permission to accompany me, saying that he was a good walker and climber and would not delay me or cause any trouble. I strongly advised him not to go, explaining that it involved a walk, coming and going, of fourteen or sixteen miles, and a climb through brush and boulders of seven thousand feet, a fair day's work for a seasoned mountaineer to be done in less than half a day and part of a night. But he insisted that he was a strong walker, could do a mountaineer's day's work in half a day, and would not hinder me in any way.

"Well, I have warned you," I said, "and will not assume responsibility for any trouble that may arise."

He proved to be a stout walker, and we made rapid progress across a brushy timbered flat and up the mountain slopes, open in some places, and in others thatched with dwarf firs, resting a minute here and there to refresh ourselves with huckleberries, which grew in abundance in open spots. About half an hour before sunset, when we were near a cluster of crumbling pinnacles that formed the summit, I had ceased to feel anxiety about the mountaineering strength and skill of my companion, and pushed rapidly on. In passing around the shoulder of the highest pinnacle, where the rock was rapidly disintegrating and the danger of slipping was great, I shouted in a warning voice, "Be very careful here, this is dangerous."

Mr. Young was perhaps a dozen or two yards behind me, but out of sight. I afterwards reproached myself for not stopping and lending him a steadying hand, and showing him the slight footsteps I had made by kicking out little blocks of the crumbling surface, instead of simply warning him to be careful. Only a few seconds after giving this warning, I was startled by a scream for help, and hurrying back, found the missionary face downward, his arms outstretched, clutching little crumbling knobs on the brink of a gully that plunges down a thousand feet or more to a small residual glacier. I managed to get below him, touched one of his feet, and tried to encourage him by saying, "I am below you. You are in no danger. You can't slip past me and I will soon get you out of this."

He then told me that both of his arms were dislocated. It was almost impossible to find available footholds on the treacherous rock, and I was at my wits' end to know how to get him rolled or dragged to a place where I could get about him, find out how much he was hurt, and a way back down the mountain. After narrowly scanning the cliff and making footholds, I managed to roll and lift him a few yards to a place where the slope was less steep, and there I attempted to set his arms. I found, however, that this was impossible in such a place. I therefore tied his arms to his sides with my suspenders and necktie, to prevent as much as possible inflammation from movement. I then left him, telling him to lie still, that I would be back in a few minutes, and that he was now safe from slipping. I hastily examined the ground and saw no way of getting him down except by the steep glacier gully. After scrambling to an outstanding point that commands a view of it from top to bottom, to make sure that it was not interrupted by sheer precipices, I concluded that with great care and the digging of slight footholds he could be slid down to the glacier, where I could lay him on his back and perhaps be able to set his arms. Accordingly, I cheered him up, telling him I had found a way, but that it would require lots of time and patience. Digging a footstep in the sand or crumbling rock five or six feet beneath him, I reached up, took hold of him by one of his feet, and gently slid him down on his back, placed his heels in the step, then descended another five or six feet, dug heel notches, and slid him down to them. Thus the whole distance was made by a succession of narrow steps at very short intervals, and the glacier was reached perhaps about midnight. Here I

took off one of my boots, tied a handker-
chief around his wrist for a good hold, placed
my heel in his arm pit, and succeeded in
getting one of his arms into place, but my
utmost strength was insufficient to reduce
the dislocation of the other. I therefore
bound it closely to his side, and asked him if
in his exhausted and trembling condition he
was still able to walk.

"Yes," he bravely replied.

So, with a steadying arm around him and
many stops for rest, I marched him slowly
down in the starlight on the comparatively
smooth, unfissured surface of the little
glacier to the terminal moraine, a distance of
perhaps a mile, crossed the moraine, bathed
his head at one of the outlet streams, and
after many rests reached a dry place and
made a brush fire. I then went ahead looking
for an open way through the bushes to where
larger wood could be had, made a good lasting fire of resiny silver-fir roots, and a leafy
bed beside it. I now told him I would run
down the mountain, hasten back with help
from the boat, and carry him down in com-
fort. But he would not hear of my leaving
him.

"No, no," he said, "I can walk down.
Don't leave me."

I reminded him of the roughness of the way, his nerve-shaken condition, and assured him I would not be gone long. But he insisted on trying, saying on no account whatever must I leave him. I therefore concluded to try to get him to the ship by short walks from one fire and resting-place to another. While he was resting I went ahead, looking for the best way through the brush and rocks, then returning, got him on his feet and made him lean on my shoulder while I steadied him to prevent his falling. This slow, staggering struggle from fire to fire lasted until long after sunrise. When at last we reached the ship and stood at the foot of the narrow single plank without side rails that reached from the bank to the deck at a considerable angle, I briefly explained to Mr. Young's companions, who stood looking down at us, that he had been hurt in an accident, and requested one of them to assist me in getting him aboard. But strange to say, instead of coming down to help, they made haste to reproach him for having gone on a "wild-goose chase" with Muir.

"These foolish adventures are well enough for Mr. Muir," they said, "but you, Mr. Young, have a work to do; you have a family; you have a church, and you have no right to

risk your life on treacherous peaks and precipices."

The captain, Nat Lane, son of Senator
Joseph Lane, had been swearing in angry impatience for being compelled to make so late
a start and thus encounter a dangerous wind
in a narrow gorge, and was threatening to put
the missionaries ashore to seek their lost companion, while he went on down the river
about his business. But when he heard my
call for help, he hastened forward, and
elbowed the divines away from the end of the
gangplank, shouting in angry irreverence,
"Oh, blank! This is no time for preaching!
Don't you see the man is hurt?"

He ran down to our help, and while I
steadied my trembling companion from behind, the captain kindly led him up the plank
into the saloon, and made him drink a large
glass of brandy. Then, with a man holding
down his shoulders, we succeeded in getting
the bone into its socket, notwithstanding the
inflammation and contraction of the muscles
and ligaments. Mr. Young was then put to
bed, and he slept all the way back to Wrangell.

In his mission lectures in the East, Mr.
Young oftentimes told this story. I made no
record of it in my notebook and never in-

tended to write a word about it; but after a miserable, sensational caricature of the story had appeared in a respectable magazine, I thought it but fair to my brave companion that it should be told just as it happened.

On the trail to the steamboat-landing at the foot of Dease Lake, I met a Douglas squirrel, nearly as red and rusty in color as his Eastern relative the chickaree. Except in color he differs but little from the California Douglas squirrel. In voice, language, gestures, temperament, he is the same fiery, indomitable little king of the woods. Another darker and probably younger specimen met near the Caribou House, barked, chirruped, and showed off in fine style on a tree within a few feet of us.

"What does the little rascal mean?" said my companion, a man I had fallen in with on the trail. "What is he making such a fuss about? I cannot frighten him."

"Never mind," I replied; "just wait until I whistle 'Old Hundred' and you will see him fly in disgust." And so he did, just as his California brethren do. Strange that no squirrel or spermophile I yet have found ever seemed to have anything like enough of Scotch religion to enjoy this grand old tune.

The taverns along the Cassiar gold trail were the worst I had ever seen, rough shacks

133

with dirt floors, dirt roofs, and rough meals. The meals are all alike — a potato, a slice of something like bacon, some gray stuff called bread, and a cup of muddy, semi-liquid coffee like that which the California miners call "slickens" or "slumgullion." The bread was terrible and sinful. How the Lord's good wheat could be made into stuff so mysteriously bad is past finding out. The very de'il, it would seem, in wicked anger and ingenuity, had been the baker.

On our walk from Dease Lake to Telegraph Creek we had one of these rough luncheons at three o'clock in the afternoon of the first day, then walked on five miles to Ward's, where we were solemnly assured that we could not have a single bite of either supper or breakfast, but as a great favor we might sleep on his best gray bunk. We replied that, as we had lunched at the lake, supper would not be greatly missed, and as for breakfast we would start early and walk eight miles to the next road-house. We set out at half-past four, glad to escape into the fresh air, and reached the breakfast place at eight o'clock. The landlord was still abed, and when at length he came to the door, he scowled savagely at us as if our request for breakfast was preposterous and criminal beyond anything ever heard of in all goldful

Alaska. A good many in those days were returning from the mines dead broke, and he
probably regarded us as belonging to that dis-
reputable class. Anyhow, we got nothing and
had to tramp on.

As we approached the next house, three
miles ahead, we saw the tavern-keeper keenly
surveying us, and, as we afterwards learned,
taking me for a certain judge whom for some
cause he wished to avoid, he hurriedly locked
his door and fled. Half a mile farther on we discovered him in a thicket a little way off the
trail, explained our wants, marched him back
to his house, and at length obtained a little
sour bread, sour milk, and old salmon, our only
lonely meal between the Lake and Telegraph
Creek.

We arrived at Telegraph Creek, the end of
my two-hundred-mile walk, about noon. After
luncheon I went on down the river to Glenora
in a fine canoe owned and manned by Kitty, a
stout, intelligent-looking Indian woman, who
charged her passengers a dollar for the fifteen-
mile trip. Her crew was four Indian paddlers.
In the rapids she also plied the paddle, with
stout, telling strokes, and a keen-eyed old man,
probably her husband, sat high in the stern and
steered. All seemed exhilarated as we shot
down through the narrow gorge on the rushing,

roaring, throttled river, paddling all the more vigorously the faster the speed of the stream, to hold good steering way. The canoe danced lightly amid gray surges and spray as if alive and enthusiastically enjoying the adventure. Some of the passengers were pretty thoroughly drenched. In unskillful hands the frail dugout would surely have been wrecked or upset. Most of the season, goods for the Cassiar gold camps were carried from Glenora to Telegraph Creek in canoes, the steamers not being able to overcome the rapids except during high water. Even then they had usually to line two of the rapids — that is, take a line ashore, make it fast to a tree on the bank, and pull up on the capstan. The freight canoes carried about three or four tons, for which fifteen dollars per ton was charged. Slow progress was made by poling along the bank out of the swiftest part of the current. In the rapids a tow line was taken ashore, only one of the crew remaining aboard to steer. The trip took a day unless a favoring wind was blowing, which often happened.

Next morning I set out from Glenora to climb Glenora Peak for the general view of the great Coast Range that I failed to obtain on my first ascent on account of the accident that befell Mr. Young when we were within a minute or two of the top. It is hard to fail in reaching a mountain-top that one starts for, let the cause be what it may. This time I had no companion to care for, but the sky was threatening. I was assured by the local weather-prophets that the day would be rainy or snowy because the peaks in sight were muffled in clouds that seemed to be getting ready for work. I determined to go ahead, however, for storms of any kind are well worth while, and if driven back I could wait and try again.

With crackers in my pocket and a light rubber coat that a kind Hebrew passenger on the steamer Gertrude loaned me, I was ready for anything that might offer, my hopes for the grand view rising and falling as the clouds rose and fell. Anxiously I watched them as they trailed their draggled skirts across the glaciers and fountain peaks as if thoughtfully looking for the places where they could do the most good. From Glenora there is first a terrace two hundred feet above the river covered mostly with bushes, yellow apocynum on the open spaces, together with carpets of dwarf manzanita, bunch-grass, and a few of the compositæ, galiums, etc. Then comes a flat stretch a mile wide, extending to the foothills, covered with birch, spruce, fir, and poplar, now mostly killed by fire and the ground strewn with

137

charred trunks. From this black forest the mountain rises in rather steep slopes covered with a luxuriant growth of bushes, grass, flowers, and a few trees, chiefly spruce and fir, the firs gradually dwarfing into a beautiful chaparral, the most beautiful, I think, I have ever seen, the flat fan-shaped plumes thickly foliaged and imbricated by snow pressure, forming a smooth, handsome thatch which bears cones and thrives as if this repressed condition were its very best. It extends up to an elevation of about fifty-five hundred feet. Only a few trees more than a foot in diameter and more than fifty feet high are found higher than four thousand feet above the sea. A few poplars and willows occur on moist places, gradually dwarfing like the conifers. Alder is the most generally distributed of the chaparral bushes, growing nearly everywhere; its crinkled stems an inch or two thick form a troublesome tangle to the mountaineer. The blue geranium, with leaves red and showy at this time of the year, is perhaps the most telling of the flowering plants. It grows up to five thousand feet or more. Larkspurs are common, with epilobium, senecio, erigeron, and a few solidagos. The harebell appears at about four thousand feet and extends to the summit, dwarfing in stature but maintaining the size of its handsome bells until they seem to be lying loose and detached on the ground as if like snow flowers they had fallen from the sky; and, though frail and delicate-looking, none of its companions is more enduring or rings out the praise of beauty-loving Nature in tones more appreciable to mortals, not forgetting even Cassiope, who also is here and her companion, Bryanthus, the loveliest and most widely distributed of the alpine shrubs. Then come crowberry, and two species of huckleberry, one of them from about six inches to a foot high with delicious berries, the other a most lavishly prolific and contented looking dwarf, few of the bushes being more than two inches high, counting to the topmost leaf, yet each bearing from ten to twenty or more large berries. Perhaps more than half the bulk of the whole plant is fruit, the largest and finest-flavored of all the huckleberries or blueberries I ever tasted, spreading fine feasts for the grouse and ptarmigan and many others of Nature's mountain people. I noticed three species of dwarf willows, one with narrow leaves, growing at the very summit of the mountain in cracks of the rocks, as well as on patches of soil, another with large, smooth leaves now turning yellow. The third species grows between the others as to elevation; its leaves, then orange-colored, are strikingly pitted and reticulated. Another alpine shrub, a species of sericocarpus, covered with handsome heads of feathery achenia, beautiful dwarf echiverias with flocks of purple flowers pricked into their bright grass-green, cushion-like bosses of moss-like foliage, and a fine forget-me-not reach to the summit. I may also mention a large mertensia, a fine anemone, a veratrum, six feet high, a large blue daisy, growing up to three to four thousand feet, and at the summit a dwarf species, with dusky, hairy involucres, and a few ferns, aspidium, gymnogramma, and small rock cheilanthes, leaving scarce a foot of ground bare, though the mountain looks bald and brown in the distance like those of the desert ranges of the Great Basin in Utah and Nevada.

Charmed with these plant people, I had almost forgotten to watch the sky until I reached the top of the highest peak, when one of the greatest and most impressively sublime of all the mountain views I have ever enjoyed came full in sight — more than three hundred miles of closely packed peaks of the great Coast Range, sculptured in the boldest manner imaginable, their naked tops and dividing ridges dark in color, their sides and the cañons, gorges, and valleys between them loaded with glaciers and snow. From this standpoint I counted upwards of two hundred glaciers, while dark-centered, luminous clouds with fringed edges hovered and crawled over them, now slowly descending, casting transparent shadows on the ice and snow, now rising high above them, lingering like loving angels guarding the crystal gifts they had bestowed. Although the range as seen from this Glenora mountain-top seems regular in its trend, as if the main axis were simple and continuous, it is, on the contrary, far from simple. In front of the highest ranks of peaks are others of the same form with their own glaciers, and lower peaks before these, and yet lower ones with their ridges and cañons, valleys and foothills. Alps rise beyond alps as far as the eye can reach, and clusters of higher peaks here and there closely crowded together; clusters, too, of needles and pinnacles innumerable like trees in groves. Everywhere the peaks seem comparatively slender and closely packed, as if Nature had here been trying to see how many noble well-dressed mountains could be crowded into one grand range.

The black rocks, too steep for snow to lie upon, were brought into sharp relief by white clouds and snow and glaciers, and these again were outlined and made tellingly plain by the rocks. The glaciers so grandly displayed are of every form, some crawling through gorge and valley like monster glittering serpents; others like broad cataracts pouring over cliffs into shadowy gulfs; others, with their main trunks winding through narrow cañons, display long, white finger-like tributaries descending from the summits of pinnacled ridges. Others lie back in fountain cirques walled in all around save at the lower edge, over which they pour in blue cascades. Snow, too, lay in folds and patches of every form on blunt, rounded ridges in curves, arrowy lines, dashes, and narrow ornamental flutings among the summit peaks and in broad, radiating wings on smooth slopes. And on many a bulging headland and lower ridge there lay heavy, over-curling copings and smooth, white domes where wind-driven snow was pressed and wreathed and packed into every form and in every possible place and condition. I never before had seen so richly sculptured a range or so many awe-inspiring inaccessible mountains crowded together. If a line were drawn east and west from the peak on which I stood, and extended both ways to the horizon, cutting the whole round landscape in two equal parts, then all of the south half would be bounded by these icy peaks, which would seem to curve around half the horizon and about twenty degrees more, though extending in a general straight, or but moderately curved, line. The deepest and thickest and highest of all this wilderness of peaks lie to the southwest. They are probably from about nine to twelve thousand feet high, springing to this elevation from near the sea-level. The peak on which these observations were made is somewhere about seven thousand feet high, and from here I estimated the height of the range. The highest peak of all, or that seemed so to me, lies to the westward at an estimated distance of about one hundred and fifty or two hundred miles. Only its solid white summit was visible. Possibly it may be the topmost peak of St. Elias. Now look northward around the other half of the horizon, and instead of countless peaks crowding into the sky, you see a low, brown region, heaving and swelling in gentle curves, apparently scarcely more waved than a rolling prairie. The so-called cañons of several forks of the upper Stickeen are visible, but even where best seen in the foreground and middle ground of the picture, they are like mere sunken gorges, making scarce perceptible marks on the landscape, while the tops of the highest mountain-swells show only small patches of snow and no glaciers.

Glenora Peak, on which I stood, is the highest point of a spur that puts out from the main range in a northerly direction. It seems to have been a rounded, broad-backed ridge which has been sculptured into its present irregular form by short residual glaciers, some of which, a mile or two long, are still at work.

As I lingered, gazing on the vast show, luminous, shadowy clouds seemed to increase in glory of color and motion, now fondling the highest peaks with infinite tenderness of touch, now hovering above them like eagles over their nests.

When night was drawing near, I ran down the flowery slopes exhilarated, thanking God for the gift of this great day. The setting sun fired the clouds. All the world seemed newborn. Every thing, even the commonest, was seen in new light and was looked at with new interest as if never seen before. The plant people seemed glad, as if rejoicing with me, the little ones as well as the trees, while every feature of the peak and its traveled boulders seemed to know what I had been about and the depth of my joy, as if they could read faces.

I STARTED off the morning of July 11 on my
memorable sled-trip to obtain general views of
the main upper part of the Muir Glacier, and
its seven principal tributaries, feeling sure that
I would learn something and at the same time
get rid of a severe bronchial cough that followed an attack of the grippe and had troubled
me for three months. I intended to camp on the
glacier every night, and did so, and my throat
grew better every day until it was well, for no
lowland microbe could stand such a trip. My
sled was about three feet long and made as
light as possible. A sack of hardtack, a little
tea and sugar, and a sleeping-bag were firmly
lashed on it so that nothing could drop off however much it might be jarred and dangled in
crossing crevasses.

Two Indians carried the baggage over the
rocky moraine to the clear glacier at the side of
one of the eastern Nunatak Islands. Mr.
Loomis accompanied me to this first camp and
assisted in dragging the empty sled over the
moraine. We arrived at the middle Nunatak
Island about nine o'clock. Here I sent back my

145

Indian carriers, and Mr. Loomis assisted me the first day in hauling the loaded sled to my second camp at the foot of Hemlock Mountain, returning the next morning.

July 13. I skirted the mountain to eastward a few miles and was delighted to discover a group of trees high up on its ragged rocky side, the first trees I had seen on the shores of Glacier Bay or on those of any of its glaciers. I left my sled on the ice and climbed the mountain to see what I might learn. I found that all the trees were mountain hemlock (*Tsuga mertensiana*), and were evidently the remnant of an old, well-established forest, standing on the only ground that was stable, all the rest of the forest below it having been sloughed off with the soil from the disintegrating slate bed rock. The lowest of the trees stood at an elevation of about two thousand feet above the sea, the highest at about three thousand feet or a little higher. Nothing could be more striking than the contrast between the raw, crumbling, deforested portions of the mountain, looking like a quarry that was being worked, and the forested part with its rich, shaggy beds of cassiope and bryanthus in full bloom, and its sumptuous cushions of flower-enameled mosses. These garden-patches are full of gay colors of gentian, erigeron, anemone, larkspur, and columbine, and are enlivened with happy birds and bees and marmots. Climbing to an elevation of twenty-five hundred feet, which is about fifteen hundred feet above the level of the glacier at this point, I saw and heard a few marmots, and three ptarmigans that were as tame as barnyard fowls. The sod is sloughing off on the edges, keeping it ragged. The trees are storm-bent from the southeast. A few are standing at an elevation of nearly three thousand feet; at twenty-five hundred feet, pyrola, veratrum, vaccinium, fine grasses, sedges, willows, mountain-ash, buttercups, and acres of the most luxuriant cassiope are in bloom.

A lake encumbered with icebergs lies at the end of Divide Glacier. A spacious, level-floored valley beyond it, eight or ten miles long, with forested mountains on its west side, perhaps discharges to the southeastward into Lynn Canal. The divide of the glacier is about opposite the third of the eastern tributaries. Another berg-dotted lake into which the drainage of the Braided Glacier flows, lies a few miles to the westward and is one and a half miles long. Berg Lake is next the remarkable Girdled Glacier to the southeastward.

When the ice-period was in its prime, much of the Muir Glacier that now flows northward into Howling Valley flowed southward into Glacier Bay as a tributary of the Muir. All the rock contours show this, and so do the medial moraines. Berg Lake is crowded with bergs because they have no outlet and melt slowly. I heard none discharged. I had a hard time crossing the Divide Glacier, on which I camped. Half a mile back from the lake I gleaned a little fossil wood and made a fire on moraine boulders for tea. I slept fairly well on the sled. I heard the roar of four cascades on a shaggy green mountain on the west side of Howling Valley and saw three wild goats fifteen hundred feet up in the steep, grassy pastures.

July 14. I rose at four o'clock this cloudy and dismal morning and looked for my goats, but saw only one. I thought there must be wolves where there were goats, and in a few minutes heard their low, dismal, far-reaching howling. One of them sounded very near and came nearer until it seemed to be less than a quarter of a mile away on the edge of the glacier. They had evidently seen me, and one or more had come down to observe me, but I was unable to catch sight of any of them. About half an hour later, while I was eating breakfast, they began howling again, so near I began to fear they had a mind to attack me, and I made haste to the shelter of a big square boulder, where, though I had no gun, I might be able to defend myself from a front attack with my alpenstock. After waiting half an hour or so to see what these wild dogs meant to do, I ventured to proceed on my journey to the foot of Snow Dome, where I camped for the night.

There are six tributaries on the northwest side of Divide arm, counting to the Gray Glacier, next after Granite Cañon Glacier going northwest. Next is Dirt Glacier, which is dead. I saw bergs on the edge of the main glacier a mile back from here which seem to have been left by the draining of a pool in a sunken hollow. A circling rim of driftwood, back twenty rods on the glacier, marks the edge of the lakelet shore where the bergs lie scattered and stranded. It is now half past ten o'clock and getting dusk as I sit by my little fossil-wood fire writing these notes. A strange bird is calling and complaining. A stream is rushing into a glacier well on the edge of which I am camped, back a few yards from the base of the mountain for fear of falling stones. A few small ones are rattling down the steep slope. I must go to bed.

July 15. I climbed the dome to plan a way, scan the glacier, and take bearings, etc., in case of storms. The main divide is about fifteen hundred feet; the second divide, about fifteen hundred also, is about one and one half miles southeastward. The flow of water on the glacier noticeably diminished last night though there was no frost. It is now already increasing. Stones begin to roll into the crevasses and into new positions, sliding against each other, half turning over or falling on moraine ridges. Mud pellets with small pebbles slip and roll slowly from ice-hummocks again and again. How often and by how many ways are boulders finished and finally brought to anything like permanent form and place in beds for farms and fields, forests and gardens. Into crevasses and out again, into moraines, shifted and reinforced and re-formed by avalanches, melting from pedestals, etc. Rain, frost, and dew help in the work; they are swept in rills, caught and ground in pot-hole mills. Moraines of washed pebbles, like those on glacier margins, are formed by snow avalanches deposited in crevasses, then weathered out and projected on the ice as shallow, raised moraines. There is one such at this camp.

A ptarmigan is on a rock twenty yards distant, as if on show. It has red over the eye, a white line, not conspicuous, over the red, belly white, white markings over the upper parts on ground of brown and black wings, mostly white as seen when flying, but the coverts the same as the rest of the body. Only about three inches of the folded primaries show white. The breast seems to have golden iridescent colors, white under the wings. It allowed me to approach within twenty feet. It walked down a sixty degree slope of the rock, took flight with a few whirring wing-beats, then sailed with wings perfectly motionless four hundred yards down a gentle grade, and vanished over the brow of a cliff. Ten days ago Loomis told me that he found a nest with nine eggs. On the way down to my sled I saw four more ptarmigans. They utter harsh notes when alarmed. "Crack, chuck, crack," with the *r* rolled and prolonged. I also saw fresh and old goat-tracks and some bones that suggest wolves.

There is a pass through the mountains at the head of the third glacier. Fine mountains stand at the head on each side. The one on the north-east side is the higher and finer every way. It has three glaciers, tributary to the third. The third glacier has altogether ten tributaries, five on each side. The mountain on the left side of White Glacier is about six thousand feet high. The moraines of Girdled Glacier seem scarce to run anywhere. Only a little material is carried to Berg Lake. Most of it seems to be at rest as a terminal on the main glacier-field, which here has little motion. The curves of these last as seen from this mountain-top are very beautiful.

It has been a glorious day, all pure sunshine. An hour or more before sunset the distant mountains, a vast host, seemed more softly ethereal than ever, pale blue, ineffably fine, all angles and harshness melted off in the soft evening light. Even the snow and the grinding, cascading glaciers became divinely tender and fine in this celestial amethystine light. I got back to camp at 7.15, not tired. After my hardtack supper I could have climbed the mountain again and got back before sunrise, but dragging the sled tires me. I have been out on the glacier examining a moraine-like mass about a third of a mile from camp. It is perhaps a mile long, a hundred yards wide, and is thickly strewn with wood. I think that it has been brought down the mountain by a heavy snow avalanche, loaded on the ice, then carried away from the shore in the direction of the flow of the glacier. This explains detached moraine-masses. This one seems to have been derived from a big roomy cirque or amphitheater on the northwest side of this Snow Dome Mountain.

To shorten the return journey I was tempted to glissade down what appeared to be a snow-filled ravine, which was very steep. All went

152

well until I reached a bluish spot which proved to be ice, on which I lost control of myself and rolled into a gravel talus at the foot without a scratch. Just as I got up and was getting myself orientated, I heard a loud fierce scream, uttered in an exulting, diabolical tone of voice which startled me, as if an enemy, having seen me fall, was glorying in my death. Then suddenly two ravens came swooping from the sky and alighted on the jag of a rock within a few feet of me, evidently hoping that I had been maimed and that they were going to have a feast. But as they stared at me, studying my condition, impatiently waiting for bone-picking time, I saw what they were up to and shouted, "Not yet, not yet!"

July 16. At 7 A.M. I left camp to cross the main glacier. Six ravens came to the camp as soon as I left. What wonderful eyes they must have! Nothing that moves in all this icy wilderness escapes the eyes of these brave birds. This is one of the loveliest mornings I ever saw in Alaska; not a cloud or faintest hint of one in all the wide sky. There is a yellowish haze in the east, white in the west, mild and mellow as a Wisconsin Indian Summer, but finer, more ethereal, God's holy light making all divine.

In an hour or so I came to the confluence of

the first of the seven grand tributaries of the main Muir Glacier and had a glorious view of it as it comes sweeping down in wild cascades from its magnificent, pure white, mountain-girt basin to join the main crystal sea, its many fountain peaks, clustered and crowded, all pouring forth their tribute to swell its grand current. I crossed its front a little below its confluence, where its shattered current, about two or three miles wide, is reunited, and many rills and good-sized brooks glide gurgling and ringing in pure blue channels, giving delightful animation to the icy solitude.

Most of the ice-surface crossed to-day has been very uneven, and hauling the sled and finding a way over hummocks has been fatiguing. At times I had to lift the sled bodily and to cross many narrow, nerve-trying, ice-sliver bridges, balancing astride of them, and cautiously shoving the sled ahead of me with tremendous chasms on either side. I had made perhaps not more than six or eight miles in a straight line by six o'clock this evening when I reached ice so hummocky and tedious I concluded to camp and not try to take the sled any farther. I intend to leave it here in the middle of the basin and carry my sleeping-bag and provisions the rest of the way across to the west side. I am cozy and comfortable here resting in the midst of glorious icy scenery, though very tired. I made out to get a cup of tea by means of a few shavings and splinters whittled from the bottom board of my sled, and made a fire in a little can, a small camp-fire, the smallest I ever made or saw, yet it answered well enough as far as tea was concerned. I crept into my sack before eight o'clock as the wind was cold and my feet wet. One of my shoes is about worn out. I may have to put on a wooden sole. This day has been cloudless throughout, with lovely sunshine, a purple evening and morning. The circumference of mountains beheld from the midst of this world of ice is marvelous, the vast plain reposing in such soft, tender light, the fountain mountains so clearly cut, holding themselves aloft with their loads of ice in supreme strength and beauty of architecture. I found a skull and most of the other bones of a goat on the glacier about two miles from the nearest land. It had probably been chased out of its mountain home by wolves and devoured here. I carried its horns with me. I saw many considerable depressions in the glacial surface, also a pitlike hole, irregular, not like the ordinary wells along the slope of the many small dirt-clad hillocks, faced to the south. Now the sun is down and the sky is saffron yellow, blending and fading into purple

155

around to the south and north. It is a curious experience to be lying in bed writing these notes, hummock waves rising in every direction, their edges marking a multitude of crevasses and pits, while all around the horizon rise peaks innumerable of most intricate style of architecture. Solemnly growling and grinding moulins contrast with the sweet, low-voiced whispering and warbling of a network of rills, singing like water-ouzels, glinting, gliding with indescribable softness and sweetness of voice. They are all around, one within a few feet of my hard sled-bed.

July 17. Another glorious cloudless day is dawning in yellow and purple and soon the sun over the eastern peak will blot out the blue peak shadows and make all the vast white ice prairie sparkle. I slept well last night in the middle of the icy sea. The wind was cold but my sleeping-bag enabled me to lie neither warm nor intolerably cold. My three-months cough is gone. Strange that with such work and exposure one should know nothing of sore throats and of what are called colds. My heavy, thick-soled shoes, resoled just before starting on the trip six days ago, are about worn out and my feet have been wet every night. But no harm comes of it, nothing but good. I suc-

ceeded in getting a warm breakfast in bed. I
reached over the edge of my sled, got hold of
a small cedar stick that I had been carrying,
whittled a lot of thin shavings from it, stored
them on my breast, then set fire to a piece of
paper in a shallow tin can, added a pinch of
shavings, held the cup of water that always
stood at my bedside over the tiny blaze with
one hand, and fed the fire by adding little
pinches of shavings until the water boiled, then
pulling my bread sack within reach, made a
good warm breakfast, cooked and eaten in
bed. Thus refreshed, I surveyed the wilderness
of crevassed, hummocky ice and concluded to
try to drag my little sled a mile or two farther,
then, finding encouragement, persevered, getting it across innumerable crevasses and streams
and around several lakes and over and through
the midst of hummocks, and at length reached
the western shore between five and six o'clock
this evening, extremely fatigued. This I consider a hard job well done, crossing so wildly
broken a glacier, fifteen miles of it from Snow
Dome Mountain, in two days with a sled weighing altogether not less than a hundred pounds.
I found innumerable crevasses, some of them
brimful of water. I crossed in most places just
where the ice was close pressed and welded
after descending cascades and was being shoved

over an upward slope, thus closing the crevasses at the bottom, leaving only the upper sun-melted beveled portion open for water to collect in.

Vast must be the drainage from this great basin. The waste in sunshine must be enormous, while in dark weather rains and winds also melt the ice and add to the volume produced by the rain itself. The winds also, though in temperature they may be only a degree or two above freezing-point, dissolve the ice as fast, or perhaps faster, than clear sunshine. Much of the water caught in tight crevasses doubtless freezes during the winter and gives rise to many of the irregular veins seen in the structure of the glacier. Saturated snow also freezes at times and is incorporated with the ice, as only from the lower part of the glacier is the snow melted during the summer. I have noticed many traces of this action. One of the most beautiful things to be seen on the glacier is the myriads of minute and intensely brilliant radiant lights burning in rows on the banks of streams and pools and lakelets from the tips of crystals melting in the sun, making them look as if bordered with diamonds. These gems are rayed like stars and twinkle; no diamond radiates keener or more brilliant light. It was perfectly glorious to think of this divine

light burning over all this vast crystal sea in
such ineffably fine effulgence, and over how
many other of icy Alaska's glaciers where nobody sees it. To produce these effects I fancy
the ice must be melting rapidly, as it was being
melted to-day. The ice in these pools does not
melt with anything like an even surface, but in
long branches and leaves, making fairy forests
of points, while minute bubbles of air are constantly being set free. I am camped to-night
on what I call Quarry Mountain from its raw,
loose, plantless condition, seven or eight miles
above the front of the glacier. I found enough
fossil wood for tea. Glorious is the view to the
eastward from this camp. The sun has set, a
few clouds appear, and a torrent rushing down
a gully and under the edge of the glacier is
making a solemn roaring. No tinkling, whis-
tling rills this night. Ever and anon I hear a
falling boulder. I have had a glorious and instructive day, but am excessively weary and
to bed I go.

July 18. I felt tired this morning and meant
to rest to-day. But after breakfast at 8 A.M.
I felt I must be up and doing, climbing, sketching new views up the great tributaries from the
top of Quarry Mountain. Weariness vanished
and I could have climbed, I think, five thou-

sand feet. Anything seems easy after sled-dragging over hummocks and crevasses, and the constant nerve-strain in jumping crevasses so as not to slip in making the spring. Quarry Mountain is the barest I have seen, a raw quarry with infinite abundance of loose, decaying granite all on the go. Its slopes are excessively steep. A few patches of epilobium make gay purple spots of color. Its seeds fly everywhere seeking homes. Quarry Mountain is cut across into a series of parallel ridges by over-sweeping ice. It is still overswept in three places by glacial flows a half to three quarters of a mile wide, finely arched at the top of the divides. I have been sketching, though my eyes are much inflamed and I can scarce see. All the lines I make appear double. I fear I shall not be able to make the few more sketches I want to-morrow, but must try. The day has been gloriously sunful, the glacier pale yellow toward five o'clock. The hazy air, white with a yellow tinge, gives an Indian-summerish effect. Now the blue evening shadows are creeping out over the icy plain, some ten miles long, with sunny yellow belts between them. Boulders fall now and again with dull, blunt booming, and the gravel pebbles rattle.

July 19. Nearly blind. The light is intoler-

able and I fear I may be long unfitted for work.
I have been lying on my back all day with a
snow poultice bound over my eyes. Every
object I try to look at seems double; even
the distant mountain-ranges are doubled, the
upper an exact copy of the lower, though somewhat faint. This is the first time in Alaska that
I have had too much sunshine. About four
o'clock this afternoon, when I was waiting for
the evening shadows to enable me to get nearer
the main camp, where I could be more easily
found in case my eyes should become still more
inflamed and I should be unable to travel, thin
clouds cast a grateful shade over all the glowing
landscape. I gladly took advantage of these
kindly clouds to make an effort to cross the few
miles of the glacier that lay between me and
the shore of the inlet. I made a pair of goggles
but am afraid to wear them. Fortunately the
ice here is but little broken, therefore I pulled
my cap well down and set off about five o'clock.
I got on pretty well and camped on the glacier
in sight of the main camp, which from here in a
straight line is only five or six miles away. I
went ashore on Granite Island and gleaned a
little fossil wood with which I made tea on the
ice.

July 20. I kept wet bandages on my eyes

last night as long as I could, and feel better this morning, but all the mountains still seem to have double summits, giving a curiously unreal aspect to the landscape. I packed everything on the sled and moved three miles farther down the glacier, where I want to make measurements. Twice to-day I was visited on the ice by a hummingbird, attracted by the red lining of the bear-skin sleeping-bag.

I have gained some light on the formation of gravel-beds along the inlet. The material is mostly sifted and sorted by successive rollings and washings along the margins of the glacier-tributaries, where the supply is abundant beyond anything I ever saw elsewhere. The lowering of the surface of a glacier when its walls are not too steep leaves a part of the margin dead and buried and protected from the wasting sunshine beneath the lateral moraines. Thus a marginal valley is formed, clear ice on one side, or nearly so, buried ice on the other. As melting goes on, the marginal trough, or valley, grows deeper and wider, since both sides are being melted, the land side slower. The dead, protected ice in melting first sheds off the large boulders, as they are not able to lie on slopes where smaller ones can. Then the next larger ones are rolled off, and pebbles and sand in succession. Meanwhile this material is subjected to torrent-action, as if it were cast into a trough. When floods come it is carried forward and stratified, according to the force of the current, sand, mud, or larger material. This exposes fresh surfaces of ice and melting goes on again, until enough material has been undermined to form a veil in front; then follows another washing and carrying-away and depositing where the current is allowed to spread. In melting, protected margin terraces are oftentimes formed. Perhaps these terraces mark successive heights of the glacial surface. From terrace to terrace the grist of stone is rolled and sifted. Some, meeting only feeble streams, have only the fine particles carried away and deposited in smooth beds; others, coarser, from swifter streams, overspread the fine beds, while many of the large boulders no doubt roll back upon the glacier to go on their travels again.

It has been cloudy mostly to-day, though sunny in the afternoon, and my eyes are getting better. The steamer Queen is expected in a day or two, so I must try to get down to the inlet to-morrow and make signal to have some of the Reid party ferry me over. I must hear from home, write letters, get rest and more to eat.

Near the front of the glacier the ice was perfectly free, apparently, of anything like a crevasse, and in walking almost carelessly down

163

it I stopped opposite the large granite Nunatak Island, thinking that I would there be partly sheltered from the wind. I had not gone a dozen steps toward the island when I suddenly dropped into a concealed water-filled crevasse, which on the surface showed not the slightest sign of its existence. This crevasse like many others was being used as the channel of a stream, and at some narrow point the small cubical masses of ice into which the glacier surface disintegrates were jammed and extended back farther and farther till they completely covered and concealed the water. Into this I suddenly plunged, after crossing thousands of really dangerous crevasses, but never before had I encountered a danger so completely concealed. Down I plunged over head and ears, but of course bobbed up again, and after a hard struggle succeeded in dragging myself out over the farther side. Then I pulled my sled over close to Nunatak cliff, made haste to strip off my clothing, threw it in a sloppy heap and crept into my sleeping-bag to shiver away the night as best I could.

July 21. Dressing this rainy morning was a miserable job, but might have been worse. After wringing my sloppy underclothing, getting it on was far from pleasant. My eyes are better and I feel no bad effect from my icy bath. The last trace of my three-months cough is gone. No lowland grippe microbe could survive such experiences.

I have had a fine telling day examining the ruins of the old forest of Sitka spruce that no great time ago grew in a shallow, mud-filled basin near the southwest corner of the glacier. The trees were protected by a spur of the mountain that puts out here, and when the glacier advanced they were simply flooded with fine sand and overborne. Stumps by the hundred, three to fifteen feet high, rooted in a stream of fine blue mud on cobbles, still have their bark on. A stratum of decomposed bark, leaves, cones, and old trunks is still in place. Some of the stumps are on rocky ridges of gravelly soil about one hundred and twenty-five feet above the sea. The valley has been washed out by the stream now occupying it, one of the glacier's draining streams a mile long or more and an eighth of a mile wide.

I got supper early and was just going to bed, when I was startled by seeing a man coming across the moraine, Professor Reid, who had seen me from the main camp and who came with Mr. Loomis and the cook in their boat to ferry me over. I had not intended making signals for them until to-morrow but was glad to go. I had been seen also by Mr. Case and one of his companions, who were on the western mountain-side above the fossil forest, shooting ptarmigans. I had a good rest and sleep and leisure to find out how rich I was in new facts and pictures and how tired and hungry I was.

Steamer Corwin,
Off Herald Island, Arctic Ocean,
July 31, 1881.

WE left Herald Island this morning at three o'clock, after landing upon it and exploring it pretty thoroughly from end to end. On the morning of the twenty-fifth we were steaming along the coast a few miles to the south of Icy Cape, intending to make an effort to reach Point Barrow in order to give aid to the whaleship Daniel Webster, which we learned was beset in the ice thereabouts and was in great danger of being lost.

We found, however, that the pack extended solidly from Icy Cape to the southward and pressed so hard against the shore that we saw it would be impossible to proceed even with the steam launch. We therefore turned back with great reluctance and came to anchor near Cape Lisburne, where we mined and took on about thirty tons of coal. About half-past four in the afternoon, July twenty-eighth, we hoisted anchor and sailed toward Herald Island, intending to make a general survey of the edge of

167

the great polar ice-pack about Wrangell Land, hardly hoping to be able to effect a landing so early in the season.

On the evening of the thirtieth we reached Herald Island, having been favored with delightful weather all the way, the ocean being calm and glassy as a mountain lake, the surface stirred gently here and there with irregular breaths of air that could hardly be called winds, and the whole of this day from midnight to midnight was all sunshine, contrasting marvelously with the dark, icy storm-days we had experienced so short a time ago.

Herald Island came in sight at one o'clock in the afternoon, and when we reached the edge of the pack it was still about ten miles distant. We made our way through it, however, without great difficulty, as the ice was mostly light and had openings of clear water here and there, though in some close-packed fields the Corwin was pretty roughly bumped, and had to steam her best to force a passage. At ten o'clock in the evening we came to anchor in the midst of huge cakes and blocks about sixty-five feet thick within two or three hundred yards of the shore.

After so many futile efforts had been made last year to reach this little ice-bound island, everybody seemed wildly eager to run ashore

and climb to the summit of its sheer granite
cliffs. At first a party of eight jumped from the
bowsprit chains and ran across the narrow belt
of margin ice and madly began to climb up an
excessively steep gully, which came to an end
in an inaccessible slope a few hundred feet
above the water. Those ahead loosened and
sent down a train of granite boulders, which
shot over the heads of those below in a far
more dangerous manner than any of the party
seemed to appreciate. Fortunately, nobody was
hurt, and all made out to get down in safety.[1]

[1] Captain Hooper's report of the incident and of Muir's
skillful ascent of the island adds some interesting details: —

"Muir, who is an experienced mountaineer, came over
the ice with an axe in his hand, and, reaching the island a few
hundred feet farther north, opposite a bank of frozen snow
and ice a hundred feet high, standing at an angle of 50°, he
deliberately commenced cutting steps and ascending the ice
cliff, the top of which he soon reached without apparent difficulty, and from there the top of the island was reached by
a gradual ascent neither difficult nor dangerous.

"While approaching the island, by a careful examination
with the glass, Muir's practiced eye had easily selected the
most suitable place for making the ascent. The place selected
by the others, or rather the place upon which they stumbled,
— for the attempt to ascend was made on the first point
reached, — was a small, steep ravine about two hundred feet
deep. The jagged nature of its steep sides made climbing
possible, and from the sea-level the top of this ravine appeared to these ambitious but inexperienced mountain-
climbers to be the top of the island. After several narrow
escapes from falling rocks they succeeded in gaining the top
of the ravine, when they discovered that the ascent was
hardly begun. Above them was a plain surface of nearly a
thousand feet in height, and so steep that the loose, disin-

While this remarkable piece of mountain-eering and Arctic exploration was in progress, a light skin-covered boat was dragged over the ice and launched on a strip of water that stretched in front of an accessible ravine, the bed of an ancient glacier, which I felt assured would conduct by an easy grade to the sum-mit of the island. The slope of this ravine for the first hundred feet or so was very steep, but inasmuch as it was full of firm, icy snow, it was easily ascended by cutting steps in the face of it with an axe that I had brought from the ship for the purpose. Beyond this there was not the slightest difficulty in our way, the glacier having graded a fine, broad road.

Kellett, who discovered this island in 1849, and landed on it under unfavorable circum-

tegrating rock with which it was covered gave way on the slightest touch and came thundering to the bottom. Some of the more ambitious were still anxious to keep on, notwith-standing the difficulty and danger, and I found it necessary to interpose my authority to prevent this useless risk of life and limb. A retreat was ordered, and with a good deal of difficulty accomplished. The descent had to be made one at a time, the upper ones remaining quiet until those below were out of danger. Fortunately, all succeeded in reaching the bottom in safety. In the mean time Muir and several others had reached the top of the island and were already searching for cairns or other signs of white men. Although the search was kept up until half-past two in the morning, nothing was found." (C. L. Hooper's *Report of the Cruise of the U.S. Revenue Steamer Thomas Corwin in the Arctic Ocean, 1881*, p. 52.)

stances, described it as "an inaccessible rock."
In general the sides are, indeed, extremely
sheer and precipitous all around, though skilled
mountaineers would find many gullies and
slopes by which they might reach the summit.
I first pushed on to the head of the glacier valley, and thence along the blackbone of the island to the highest point, which I found to be
about twelve hundred feet above the level of
the sea. This point is about a mile and a half
from the northwest end, and four and a half
from the northeast end, thus making the island about six miles in length. It has been cut
nearly in two by the glacial action it has under-
gone, the width at the lowest portion being
about half a mile, and the average width about
two miles.

The entire island is a mass of granite, with
the exception of a patch of metamorphic slate
near the center, and no doubt owes its existence, with so considerable a height, to the
superior resistance this granite offered to the
degrading action of the northern ice-sheet,
traces of which are here plainly shown, as well
as on the shores of Siberia and Alaska and down
through Bering Strait southward beyond Van-
couver Island. Traces of the subsequent partial glaciation to which it has been subjected
are also manifested in glacial valleys of con-

siderable depth as compared with the size of
the island. I noticed four of these, besides many
marginal glacial grooves around the sides. One
small remnant [of a glacier] with feeble action
still exists near the middle of the island. I also
noted several scored and polished patches on
the hardest and most enduring of the outswell-
ing rock-bosses. This little island, standing as
it does alone out in the Polar Sea, is a fine glacial monument.

The midnight hour I spent alone on the
highest summit — one of the most impressive
hours of my life. The deepest silence seemed
to press down on all the vast, immeasurable,
virgin landscape. The sun near the horizon
reddened the edges of belted cloud-bars near
the base of the sky, and the jagged ice-boulders
crowded together over the frozen ocean stretching indefinitely northward, while perhaps a
hundred miles of that mysterious Wrangell
Land was seen blue in the northwest — a wavering line of hill and dale over the white and blue
ice-prairie! Pale gray mountains loomed beyond, well calculated to fix the eye of a mountaineer. But it was to the far north that I ever
found myself turning, to where the ice met the
sky. I would fain have watched here all the
strange night, but was compelled to remember
the charge given me by the Captain, to make

haste and return to the ship as soon as I should find it possible, as there was ten miles of shifting, drifting ice between us and the open sea.

I therefore began the return journey about one o'clock this morning, after taking the compass bearings of the principal points within sight on Wrangell Land, and making a hasty collection of the flowering plants on my way. I found one species of poppy quite showy, and making considerable masses of color on the sloping uplands, three or four species of saxifrage, one silene, a draba, dwarf willow, stellaria, two golden compositæ, two sedges, one grass, and a veronica, together with a considerable number of mosses and lichens, some of them quite showy and so abundant as to furnish most of the color over the gray granite.

Innumerable gulls and murres breed on the steep cliffs, the latter most abundant. They kept up a constant din of domestic notes. Some of them are sitting on their eggs, others have young, and it seems astonishing that either eggs or the young can find a resting-place on cliffs so severely precipitous. The nurseries formed a lively picture — the parents coming and going with food or to seek it, thousands in rows standing on narrow ledges like bottles on a grocer's shelves, the feeding of the little ones, the multitude of wings, etc.

173

Foxes were seen by Mr. Nelson [1] near the top of the northeast end of the island, and after we had all returned to the ship and were getting under way, the Captain discovered a polar bear swimming deliberately toward the ship between some floating blocks within a few yards of us. After he had approached within about a dozen yards the Captain shot at him, when he turned and made haste to get away, not diving, however, but swimming fast, and keeping his head turned to watch the ship,

[1] In a recent article on "The Larger North American Mammals" Mr. E. W. Nelson has given the following account of this incident: —

"The summer of 1881, when we landed from the Corwin on Herald Island, northwest of Bering Straits, we found many white foxes living in burrows under large scattered rocks on the plateau summit. They had never seen men before and our presence excited their most intense interest and curiosity. One and sometimes two of them followed closely at my heels wherever I went, and when I stopped to make notes or look about, sat down and watched me with absurd gravity. Now and then one at a distance would mount a rock to get a better view of the stranger.

"On returning to the ship, I remembered that my notebook had been left on a large rock over a fox den, on the island, and at once went back for it. I had been gone only a short time, but no trace of the book could be found on or about the rock, and it was evident that the owner of the den had confiscated it. Several other foxes sat about viewing my search with interest and when I left followed me to the edge of the island. A nearly grown young one kept on the Corwin was extraordinarily intelligent, inquisitive, and mischievous, and afforded all of us much amusement and occasional exasperation." (*National Geographic Magazine*, November, 1916, p. 425.)

until at length he received a ball in the neck and stained the blue water with his blood. He was a noble-looking animal and of enormous strength, living bravely and warm amid eternal ice.

We looked carefully everywhere for traces of the crew of the Jeannette along the shore, as well as on the prominent headlands and cliffs about the summit, without discovering the faintest sign of their ever having touched the island.

We have been steaming along the edge of the pack all day after reaching open water, with Wrangell Land constantly in sight; but we find that the ice has been sheering us off farther and farther from it toward the west and south. The margin of the main pack has a jagged saw-tooth outline, the teeth being from two to ten miles or more in length, and their points reaching about forty miles from the shore of Wrangell Land. Our chances, however, of reaching this mysterious country some time this year seem good at present, as the ice is melting fast and is much lighter than usual, and its wind and current movements, after it breaks up, will be closely watched for an available opening.